About the Author

Ian Korf is a Professor of Bioinformatics and Genomics at the University of California Davis. No, this has nothing to do with racing or cars.

Acknowledgements

I want to say thanks (and sorry) to my wife for her patience with my pastime. I never imagined I was going to spend so many weekends working on racecars. Thanks to Thomas Ulrich for showing me how to turn a wrench and to Ben Dawson for showing me how to unwrench a turn. I have my twin brother Mario to blame for getting the ball rolling and Daniel Melters, Derek Stotz, David DeFlyer, and Bill Manofsky for keeping it rolling.

Thanks to Murilee Martin for the cover photo and to the following companies who gave permission to reproduce images of their products: Autosport Labs, Fresh Air Systems Technologies, iRacing Motorsport Simulations, Necksgen, RumbleStrip Racing Products, StaCool, Track Systems Technologies, and Z-Tech Sports.

Introduction

At the American Museum of Natural History in New York City, there is an exhibit titled "How to get bitten by a snake". It's a cute diorama featuring multiple ways to put yourself in danger of getting bitten by a snake. At 10 years old, my imaginative mind thought every snake was a rattlesnake or cobra, so it made an indelible impression. To this day, I'm still wary of where I put my unprotected hands and feet. For some reason, a message saying "here's how to be stupid" has a greater effect than "don't be stupid". Maybe it's because people don't like to be told what to do and automatically rebel against authority. Or maybe that's just me.

In 2007, when webisodes were a new entertainment media, one of my favorites was called "You Suck At Photoshop". It follows the humorously tragic life of "Donny Hoyle", a digital artist with amazing skill at editing digital images and ineptitude at personal relationships. I watched it for the humor but accidentally became educated in layers, transforms, colors, etc. The series succeeds at being both entertaining and subversively educational. I admire it greatly.

In 2014, I started a blog called *you suck at racing: a crash course in auto racing*, which finds itself at the intersection of "How to get bitten by a snake", "You Suck At Photoshop" and my own performance-driving self-education journey. The blog features video clips of crashes and post-crash analysis in an admittedly snarky tone. This book is the companion to that, focusing more on what to do than what not to do, and with less snark and more bark.

Unlike most track junkies, I'm not very passionate about cars. I didn't grow up around cars, racing, or wrenching, and I've never followed motorsports as a fan. There's a part of me that doesn't even *approve* of sports cars because of how impractical and expensive they are. I got interested in road racing because my brother told me that racecars that compete in the 24 Hours of LeMons are only $500. Split 6 ways it seemed like a bargain at $83. Little did I know that my neck brace was going to set me back $600... Fast forward a few years and racing is now my main hobby. What won me over was not the fast cars or historic tracks, but the *driving*. There is no greater joy than delicately balancing a racecar at the limit (except for the occasional trespass and safe return from well beyond).

A lot of books on driving are written by professional racers who assume you too want to be a professional racer. Not this book. It's written by a hobbyist who suggests you keep your day job. Besides, it's much more fun being an enthusiastic amateur than a jaded professional (just ask someone in the sex industry). This book is designed to help the average driver make the transition from commuter to safe road racer in as few pages as possible.

I wrote this book because it's what I would have wanted to read when I first became interested in track driving: succinct, nerdy, practical, and occasionally diverting. It is not intended as a definitive tome or a work of art. It's more like a sandwich: convenient and nourishing. You will find quotes and references throughout that point to other sources of driving instruction. I suspect you will want dinner sometime after lunch. Oh, and just in case you think I'm delusional about being a racing authority, I fully accept that I suck at racing. I only claim to suck a lot less than I used to.

There are several really important things missing from this book. There is very little information about building/tuning cars, running a team, racing strategy, or coordinating activities during a race -- you know, the things that actually determine if you're going to win or not. There's a lot more that I could have written about driver development and data analysis too. But this is a crash course for the novice driver, with an emphasis on *novice* and *driver*.

Racing isn't for everyone. It's a little more expensive, exclusive, wasteful, irresponsible, and dangerous than most other sports. So why do it? You'll find a lot of reasons among racers: aesthetics, bravado, competition, danger, engineering, friendships, glory, history... I have my own reason: it makes me feel alive.

A ship in harbor is safe, but that is not what ships are built for.

-- John A. Shedd

A is for Apex

It's better to go into a corner slow and come out fast than it is to go into a corner fast and come out dead.

-- Sir Sterling Moss

The Racing Line

You will hear a lot of drivers talk about what **line** they take through a particular corner. It's not something painted on the track! The line is simply the path the car takes through a corner, and there are many possible paths, including those that go off track and mow the lawn. Let's consider the shortest path first. Assuming a right-hand turn as shown in **Figure A.1**, the shortest path, marked **A**, travels along the inside edge of the corner.

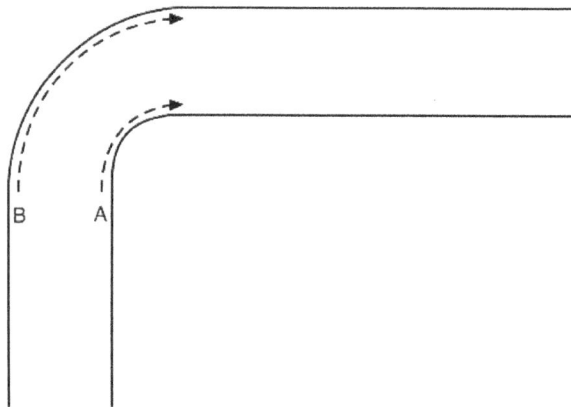

Figure A.1: A Typical Corner

Being the shortest path, it takes the least time to travel, on foot anyway. But is this also true in a racecar? There is a very simple equation that relates velocity, grip, and radius. If math isn't your forte, don't panic. There are only a couple equations in this book and they are all pretty simple once you get to know them.

The velocity (V) depends on the grip (G) of the tires and the radius (R) of the turn. Grippier tires allow you to go faster. We can't change our tires while driving, but we can change the radius of the turn. So let's forget about tires and focus on radius. A larger radius raises corner speed, but it's not linear. Twice the radius isn't twice the speed. If we double the radius, this will increase the speed by the square-root of 2, which is approximately 1.4. So if we go 10 mph around the corner on the inside of the turn, we can go 14 mph on an arc that is twice as large, which is path **B** in the figure. So path **B** is twice as long and the speed is only 1.4 times as high, which means it takes longer to take path **B** than **A** whether we're walking or driving.

While path **A** has the advantage of being the quickest way through the corner by virtue of having the shortest distance, it has one huge disadvantage: it has the lowest speed at the end of the turn. Usually, a corner is followed by a straight, and the straights are where most passing happens. In order to overtake another car, you need a good exit speed. Driving a larger radius means you spend more time in the corner, but you exit with a higher speed. Does that mean path **B** is better? Not necessarily. Thankfully there are a lot more lines than just **A** and **B**.

The Geometric Line

The largest radius through the turn is path **C** shown in **Figure A.2**. This **geometric line** is a circular arc that starts on the outside of the track, continues to the inside, and then back to the outside. This creates a path with the largest radius and therefore highest speed. The point at which you begin to turn the steering wheel is called the **entry** or **turn in**. This is at the outside edge of the track. The **apex** is the point closest to the inside of the track. The **exit** or **track out** is where you are closest to the outside edge of the track.

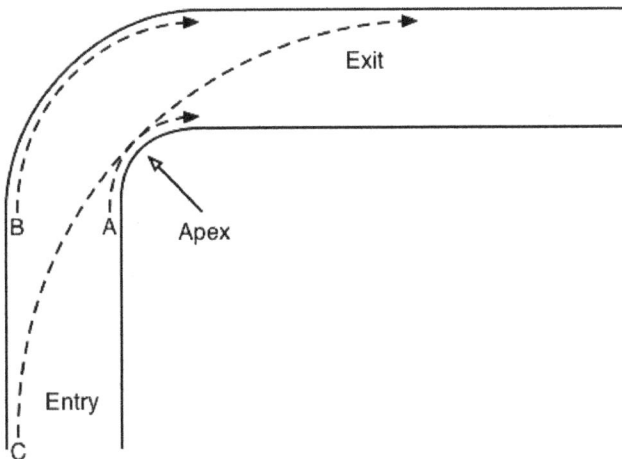

Figure A.2: The Ideal Line

Let's compare arc **C** with arcs **A** and **B**. The table below shows the the radius, distance traveled, and corner speed assuming tires with 1.0g grip. The geometric line is only a little longer than the shortest path and has over twice the speed.

Arc	Radius	Distance	Corner Speed
A	100 ft	617 ft	38.6 mph
B	200 ft	774 ft	54.6 mph
C	430 ft	675 ft	80.1 mph

This simple analysis has a problem, however. It ignores the speed on the straight sections before and after **A** and **B**. In a powerful car with good brakes, you can take the inside line, clog the corner, and rocket away on the following straight. Mustangs do this to Miatas all the time. It's called cheating (says the Miata-owning author). More seriously, powerful cars benefit just as much from a larger radius as momentum cars.

The Late Apex

The **optimal line**, which is the one gets you around the track the fastest, is generally not the geometric line above. The most obvious feature of the optimal line is a **late apex**. **Figure A.3** shows the optimal line as path **D**. As you can see, the apex is past the halfway point through the turn. The radius of the turn from entry to apex is shorter than the ideal line and the entry speed must therefore be lower (as we saw from the equation above). While this may seem disadvantageous on the surface, it is actually faster because you can turn the exit of the corner into a drag strip.

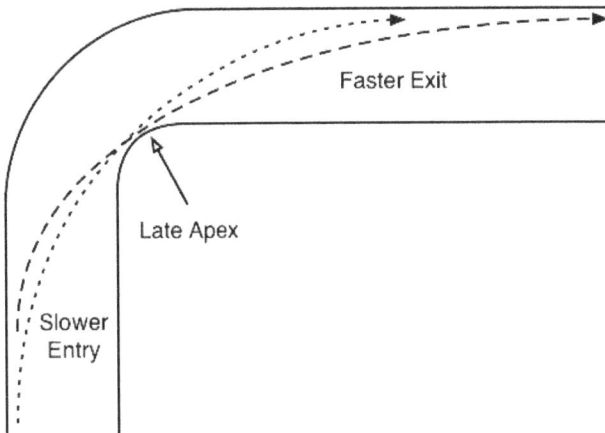

Figure A.3: The Optimal Line

When in doubt, drive a late apex. In addition to being generally faster, it's also safer because you have a lower speed earlier in the corner so you have more time to fix mistakes if you mess up. The humorous adage "get behind early, that way you have more time to catch up" actually makes sense in this instance. Here are a few rules of thumb for finding the late apex of a corner.

- The more powerful the car, the later the apex
- The tighter the corner, the later the apex
- The lower the traction, the later the apex
- The more unfamiliar the track, the later the apex
- The more expensive the car, the later the apex
- The smaller the bank account, the later the apex

Cars with front-wheel drive also take a later apex. The reason is that when you accelerate, the weight of the car shifts rearward. So the drive wheels have lower traction. In order to accelerate efficiently, you want to get the car pointed straight as soon as possible, and this means taking a late apex line.

B is for Braking

It is amazing how many drivers, even at the Formula 1 level, think that the brakes are for slowing the car down.

-- Mario Andretti

Although mechanically simple, your brakes are one of the most important parts of your car and braking is one the most important skills you can learn. Brakes are not only your safety net, they are also the key to speed.

Threshold Braking

Slowing your car from over 100 mph to exactly 40 mph is not something you have to do in a street car, but is very common on a race track. Bringing your speed down as quickly as possible while maintaining control is called **threshold braking**. The fastest way to stop a car is not stomping on the pedal as hard as possible while your tires scream and smoke. A smoking tire has poor traction because rubber loses grip if it gets too hot (see "R is for Rubber"). If you lock your wheels, you can also develop a flat spot on your tires. Once this happens, every time you brake your tires will settle into the same flat spot making it worse and worse. Not only does this mean you have to replace your tires sooner, the flat spots affect handling and make an annoying thump-thump-thump as you drive.

The reason threshold braking is difficult is because tires have their maximum grip when they are sliding a little bit. In Physics class, you may have learned that the coefficient of static friction is greater than the coefficient of dynamic friction. But tires aren't metal blocks sliding down wooden ramps. Rubber is a viscoelastic compound with some really strange properties, and one of those properties is that there is more grip when the tires are sliding than when they are stationary. Too much sliding and you end up with a flat spot though. Too little sliding and you're not using all the traction available. **Modulating brake pedal pressure** so that your tires are rotating just the right amount for optimal grip is a difficult skill to master, especially since the pressure changes subtly through the braking zone.

Some people have the bad habit of braking gently at first and then increasing pressure as they slow down. This is unsafe and slow. If you make your braking zone too long, people in back of you may try to pass you just before the corner entry. Also, if you need to make an emergency maneuver, it's better to do this at a slower speed. So getting rid of your speed quickly is better than gradually.

To stop in the shortest distance, you need to get to optimal brake pressure as quickly as possible. Of course, you have to do this without overheating and damaging your tires. It's difficult and takes lots of practice, just like a critical skill in any sport. **Figure B.1.** shows what initial braking pressure should look like over time. Line A shows what you're supposed to do. Line B is what many novices do.

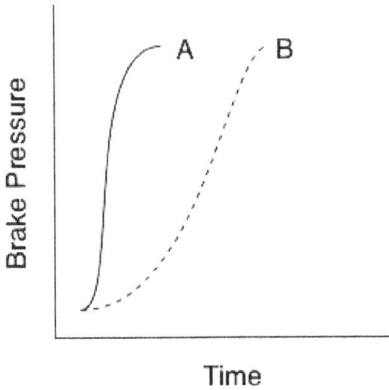

Figure B.1: Initial Brake Pressure

Trail-Braking

Trail-braking is the act of gradually releasing brake pressure while turning into a corner. Novices are generally taught to separate braking from turning because the mixture may cause you to spin. To me, that's sort of like teaching someone to swim outside of water because you might drown. It's not a good idea to throw a novice swimmer into the deep end of the pool, and it's not a good idea to tell a novice driver to trail-brake on the fastest turn of the track.

So how do you begin? Start by braking in a straight line, but more gently. Don't stomp on the brake pedal and don't snap off it. Sudden motions disrupt the balance of the car. **Figure B.2** graphs the difference between trail-braking (**A**) and snapping off the brake (**B**).

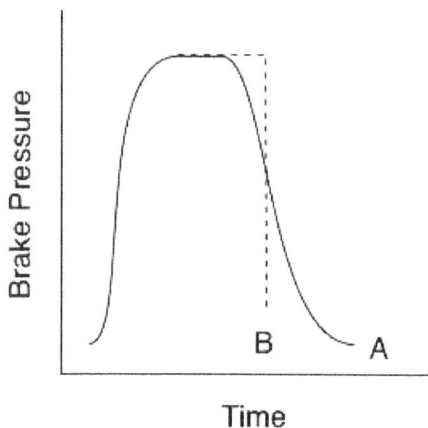

Figure B.2: Trail-Braking

Focus on what it feels like to release the brake pedal gradually. After you're comfortable with that, start turning the steering wheel a little just before the brake is fully released. That's trail-braking! It's really not complicated. Try this at slow speeds and gradually build up to the point where you feel the rear tires start to slide out a little. Then open the wheel or release some brake and you will regain grip and stop sliding. It's critical for you to learn how to sense and control grip so that you don't spin. Unless you repeatedly put yourself in about-to-spin situations, you will never learn how to control a car at the limit. Note that it's much easier to practice trail-braking on hard street tires than race tires, and much safer to practice in slow corners than fast ones.

There are several good reasons to trail-brake. (1) You can brake later because you extend the braking zone into the turn. (2) You can rotate the car earlier in the corner and get on the gas sooner. (3) You can *feel* how fast you're going by how much the self-aligning torque of the tires tugs at the steering wheel in your hands. While reasons 1 & 2 will lower your lap times, reason 3 is the best reason to trail-brake. By feeling your speed, you can set your entry speed more accurately, which makes you both faster and safer. It takes a long time to train yourself to feel your speed, but this skill is one of the most important skills in racing.

People who don't trail-brake have a misconception about the technique and/or the purpose. It is not applying your brakes mid-corner. That's called fail-braking and it leads to accidents. It's important to understand that even when trail-braking, the majority of the slowing down is done in a straight line. Trail-braking is something that is done towards the end of a braking zone. The most important reason to trail-brake is that it let's you feel the road with your hands. But it also lets you turn the car with weight transfer rather than the steering wheel. I believe that's what Mario Andretti was talking about in the quote that starts the chapter.

Entry Speed

Between two equally matched cars, the one with the faster speed on the straights generally wins because the straights are longer and higher speed. So there is obviously a lot of focus on the exit speed of a corner. But if the speed on the straights is determined by the exit speed, what does the exit speed depend on? Mid-corner speed. And what does mid-corner speed depend on? Entry speed. And what does entry speed depend on? Your braking technique. If you enter a corner too fast, you may end up off track. If you enter too slow, there's no way to get back the speed you lost. Despite appearances, the brake pedal is the go-fast pedal.

Brake Bias and ABS

Some racecars are equipped with a proportioning valve that lets you adjust how much brake pressure goes to the front and how much to the rear. Sometimes these prop valves are even adjustable from the cockpit. Messing around with your **brake bias** is an excellent way to understand how weight transfer affects the handling of your car. But it can be dangerous if done incorrectly. If you have too much rear brakes, you can spin very easily, even when braking in a straight line. If you have too much front brakes, the car will require a longer braking zone. Many a racecar has been destroyed from improperly proportioned brakes.

If your track car has an anti-lock braking system (ABS), don't remove it. Expert racers can stop their cars in a shorter distance without ABS, but you're not a professional racer (and if you are, why are you reading this book?). ABS will save you money by preventing you (and others who drive your car) from flat-spotting your tires. ABS also reduces the chance you will spin into another car or into a wall. That's worth a lot more than a couple of feet of braking distance. But if you have ABS, that doesn't give you license to stomp on and snap off the brake pedal. Smoothness still rules the day.

Left Foot Braking

Braking with your left foot (**LFB**) has some advantages. It allows you to transition more quickly from braking to throttle and to do it more smoothly if you've practiced it a lot. There are even cases where using both pedals at the same time is useful. Go-karts and simulators are a good way to practice LFB. The street is the wrong place. LFB is an advanced skill, not necessarily because it's difficult to do, but because the effect is small. Until you're at the point where tenths of a second matter, LFB is not worth the trouble.

Engine Braking

Downshifting and using the clutch and engine to slow the car is generally a bad idea in a racecar. Not only does it put extra wear on the clutch, it also changes the brake bias either forward or rearward depending on which wheels have power. If you engine-brake, congrats, you just made your braking distance longer. Also, with your bias artificially out of adjustment, you may find yourself understeering or oversteering off track and into a wall.

Hand Brake

There isn't much use for the hand brake in road racing. The exception is a front-wheel drive car with a lot of understeer. Adding a little extra rear wheel brake bias can be useful in that case. But it's better to adjust the car and keep two hands on the wheel.

C is for Corners

Straight roads are for fast cars, turns are for fast drivers.

-- Colin McRae

Corners

In Alan Johnson's famous book *Driving in Competition*, he codifies the 3 types of corners.

- **Type 1**: slow in, fast out
- **Type 2**: fast in, slow out
- **Type 3**: everything else (compromises)

Type 1 corners are the simplest and most important. Type 2 corners are uncommon, difficult, and dangerous. Type 3 corners are the most fun.

Type 1 Corners

One of the common phrases you hear from driving coaches is "slow in, fast out". That describes the strategy of a Type 1 corner (**Figure C.1**) The most important part of the corner is not really the corner, but the high speed straight that follows it. If a corner isn't followed by a long straight, it's not a Type 1 corner. Because the exit speed is crucial, the racing line must optimize exit speed, and the shape is therefore a late apex line (see "A is for Apex"). Arriving at the exit at the highest speed depends on hitting the slowest part of the corner at the correct speed (see "B is for Brakes") and angle (see "N is for Nadir").

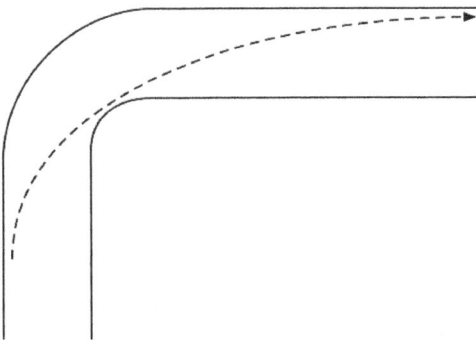

Figure C.1: Type 1 Corner

Type 2 Corners

Type 2 corners start with a long straight and are followed by a much slower section. The slowness might be a tight corner, a short straight, an off-camber turn, or traffic. Whatever the case, your exit speed is not the most important factor, so the line does not trace a late apex. You're approaching with high speed and you want to keep that speed for as long as possible. That means serious threshold braking through an early apex. The best way to think about this type of corner is 3 separate phases (**Figure C.2**). The typical late apex line is shown as a dashed line for comparison.

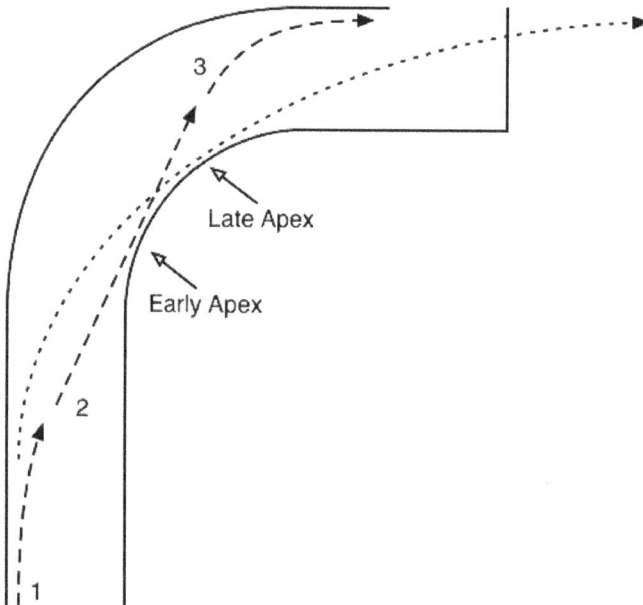

Figure C.2: Type 2 Corner

1. Turn the car towards the apex under throttle. You don't have to be anywhere near 100% throttle, but some throttle will help stabilize the car. If you need to scrub off some speed, do it on the straight *before* you turn in. Lifting off the throttle or braking in a high speed turn is one of the best ways to spin off track and wreck your car (see "O is for Oversteer").

2. Threshold brake in a straight line all the way to the apex. Everything happens more quickly at high speed, and trying to make steering adjustments during high speed braking is not recommended. This is why straight-line braking is preferred

over trail-braking here. Once the car has zero side-loading and the suspension is quiet, you can begin aggressive threshold braking. Ideally you're pointed directly at the apex, but it's better to miss the apex than to brake too late.

3. As your speed decreases, trail-brake to rotate the car and finish the turn. If done correctly, it will feel like you completely ruined the exit, which you did. But it was for a good cause: time.

Type 3 Corners

Type 3 corners don't have long straights before or after them. They are often found in a group, and they can be complicated by elevation or camber. Type 3 corners are the least important to get right because there isn't much time to be gained and passing opportunities are rare. But they are the most important not to get wrong because you could end up off track if you get off line or out of rhythm.

The typical Type 3 corner is a right-left or left-right combination. The first corner is the Type C corner. As shown in **Figure C.3**, you have to sacrifice the usual track out at the exit in order to set up for the much more important section that follows.

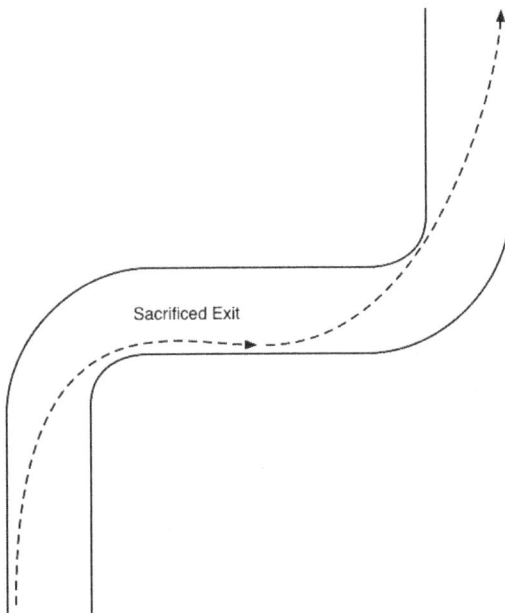

Sacrificed Exit

Figure C.3: Type 3 Corner

Connected Corners: Hairpins, Carousels & Double 90s

Let's examine two connected corners and see how they interact with each other. For simplicity, let's assume there are long straights both before and after the corners. **Figures C.4 - C.6** show two 90° corners separated by a variable amount of straight.

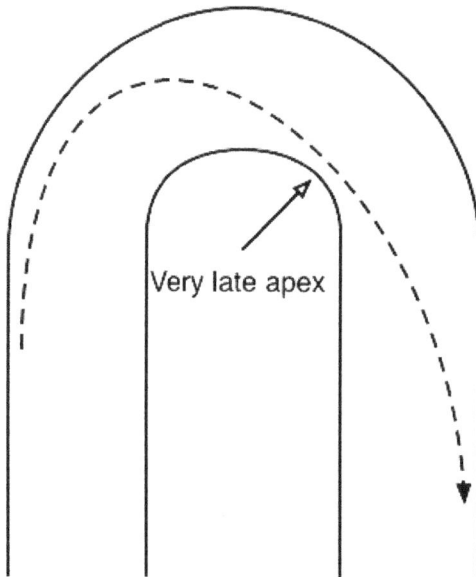

Figure C.4: Hairpin

The line in **Figure C.4** is a single very late apex. The entry is wide and slow, and most of the rotation is done well before the apex.

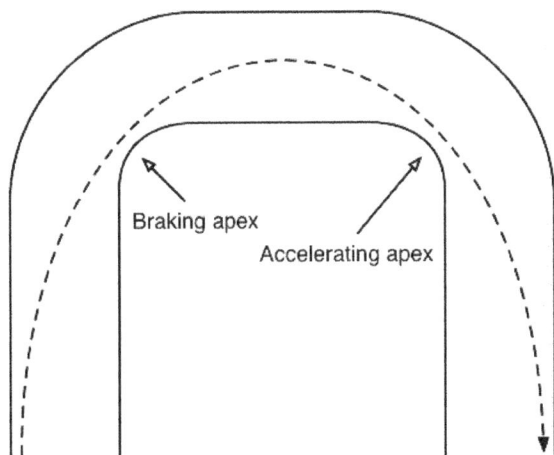

Figure C.5: Double Apex

The line in **Figure C.5** is a double-apex. The first apex is taken under braking while the second apex is taken with throttle on. Corners like this are often called *carousels*.

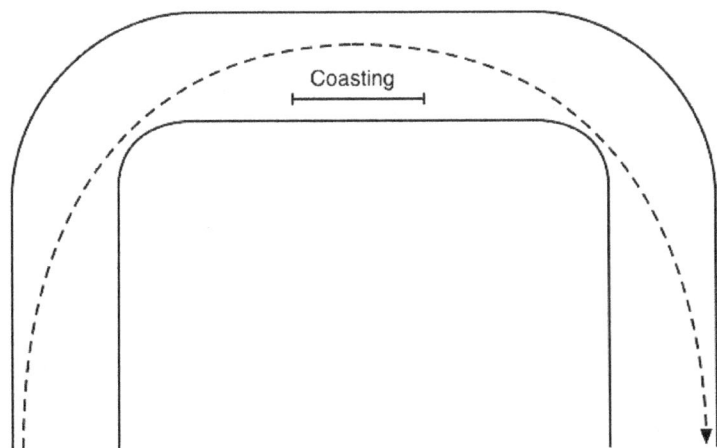

Figure C.6: Tweener

The line in **Figure C.6** is complicated by the uncomfortably long distance between the two turns. If the distance was shorter, the line would be a double apex. If the distance was longer, the turns would have their own separate braking zone, entry, apex, and exit. If you try to take this as 2 turns, you will end up using throttle and brake in the middle section. This back-and-forth upsets the suspension and complicates your driving. The alternative is to treat this as a double apex with some coasting in the middle. **Coasting** doesn't necessarily mean zero throttle but rather not aggressively accelerating. In some turns you may be at zero throttle and others 10%. Keep the car balanced, and when you go to the throttle in earnest, go there just once.

Chicanes & Esses

When two corners are connected and change directions, they form either a **chicane** or an **esse** (**Figure C.7**).

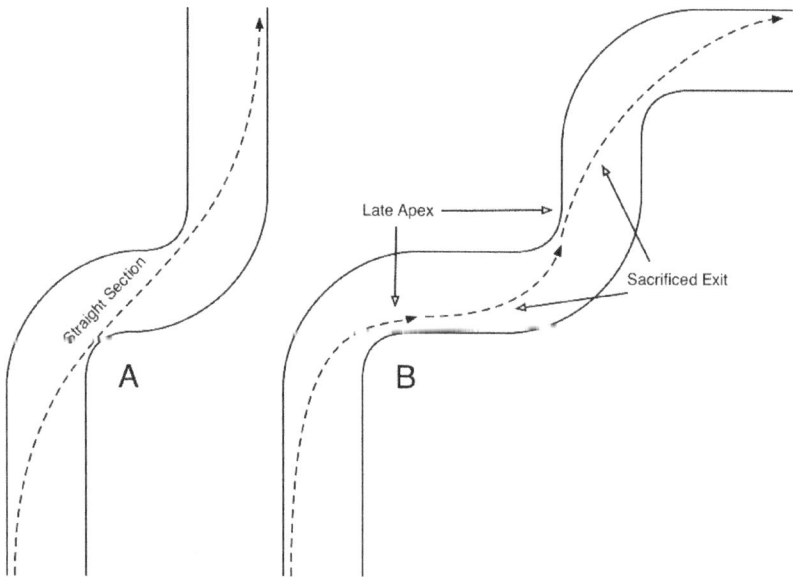

Figure C.7: Chicane

A shows a chicane. The main difficulty in a chicane is that the quick side-to-side change in direction can imbalance the car. So it's important to be very smooth and to minimize turning through the middle. Try to straighten it out as much as possible, but put more emphasis on the exit than the entrance. If the track uses tires to mark the chicane, steer clear because they can damage your car. Steer clear of berms too, because a quick side-to-side weight transfer mixed with a berm can send your car into a rollover.

B shows a series of esses. Esses are type C corners that require you to repeatedly sacrifice the exit to set up for the next entry. If you run wide on the exit, you will completely ruin the next entry. Not only will this kill your lap time, you may be forced to run off track. Esses typically require no braking as speed is continually being rubbed off from changes in direction. How much throttle you add at various points through the turns is critical. Too much can throw you off track and the knee-jerk response to over-speeding is lifting completely off the throttle. This can lead to a spin (see "O is for Oversteer"). The key is to stay in rhythm and not overspeed.

Increasing and Decreasing Radius Corners

Both increasing and decreasing radius turns are challenging because you can't simply make the car **take a set** and then drive around at constant speed.

In **Figure C.8**, panel **A** shows an increasing radius turn. The most important feature of these turns is that the turn goes faster the longer you are in it. So get the slow parts over with quickly and then get on the gas as early and strong as traction allows. These turns aren't particularly dangerous, but they are difficult to optimize in a powerful car as you mix throttle and steering.

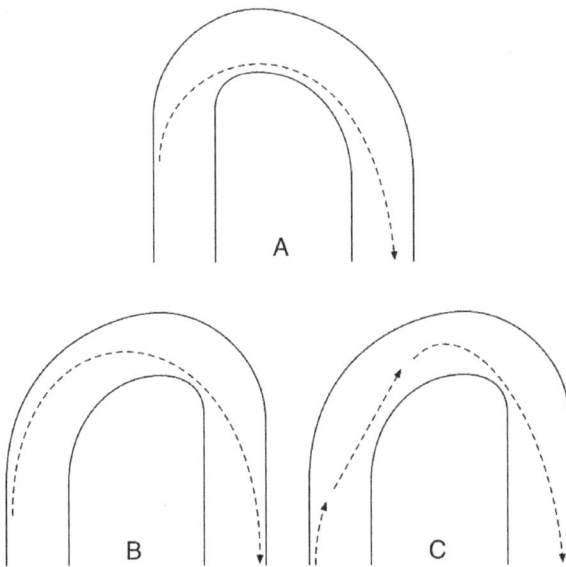

Figure C.8: Increasing & Decreasing Radius

Panel **B** shows a decreasing radius turn. These are some of the most misunderstood turns. The knee-jerk response of a novice driver is to brake in a straight line, turn in, and get on the gas. The problem is that about half-way through the turn the driver thinks "this is easy" and then runs off the track at the exit as the radius tightens up. "Slow in fast out" is actually dangerous here. The key to this turn is trail-braking because it let's you brake later, maintain speed through the corner, and gradually reduce your speed until you reach the apex.

If you don't feel confident about your trail-braking skills or your car is mis-tuned to oversteer as soon as you touch the brakes, you need an alternate strategy. Panel **C** shows how you can turn a decreasing radius turn into a Type 2 corner. That is, turn the car in towards the apex under power, brake through the apex in a straight line, and then recover at slow speed on the other side.

D is for Driving Position

Cure sometimes, treat often, comfort always.

-- Hippocrates

Seat

In general, you want the seat to be a little closer and a little more vertical than the seat in your street car. The seat should be positioned forward enough that your elbows and knees are slightly bent but not so forward that you feel cramped.

The closer the steering wheel is to your body, the more control you will have. If you watch NASCAR drivers, you'll see their steering wheels are practically in their chests and their forearms may be resting on the wheel. NASCAR drivers require the utmost feel while they slide around the track, and they also don't want to get tired. A close steering wheel solves both problems. The old pictures of Formula 1 drivers with their arms straight out are just that, old. To bring your steering wheel closer, you may need a hub extender. Add a quick release hub to make entry and egress easier.

Your legs should be relaxed with enough room to push the pedals all the way to the floor. If you're too cramped up, it can get uncomfortable for a long driving stint.

Some racing seats have zero padding. This might be tolerable for a 20 minute session, but is a real hindrance in an endurance race. You want your attention on the driving, not on how much your back hurts. So put some foam in your seat if it doesn't have enough.

Pedals

The brake pedal should be higher than the throttle so that when it is fully depressed it is still higher than the throttle (see "H is for Heel-Toe"). If you brake with your left foot (or want to learn) you may need a wider brake pedal. The position of the clutch pedal is not critical, but it should not be in the way of the brake if you use your left foot. In addition to the typical 3 pedals, you should also have a dead pedal to provide support when corning. Your heels should remain anchored on the floor at all times because this helps your fine muscle control.

Hands

For best control, your hands should be placed on opposite sides of the wheel. Some people grip at 9-and-3 while others grip at 10-and-2 or 8-and-4. The supports of your steering wheel can get in the way of your preferred position, in which case you may want a different wheel. Find a position that feels good and then *leave your hands there.*

Road racing tracks are not like parking lots or autocross courses. There is very little need to rotate the steering wheel more than 180°. You can turn the wheel at least 180° without removing your hands from the wheel. So leave them there. No hand-over-hand steering. No palming the wheel. **Two hands, opposite sides of the wheel, all the time.**

Shuffle steering is the act of moving your hands around the wheel while you turn it. Your first driving instructor may have taught you to do this to prevent you from tying your arms in a knot. They won't, and there's nothing wrong with crossing your arms. One very common problem with shuffle steering is drivers losing control of the wheel when trying to recover from oversteer.

You should grip the wheel with a light but firm touch. The front wheels have a lot to communicate with you, and you can't hear what they're saying if you're holding onto the wheel with a death grip. Hold the steering wheel like you're holding hands with a loved one while crossing the street. Feel the car through your fingers.

Eyes

What people call serendipity sometimes is just having your eyes open.

--Jose Manuel Barroso

Your eyes contain a mixture of photoreceptors called cones and rods. Cones are mostly in the center of your eyes and are responsible for color vision. Rods are located more on the periphery and only see in black and white. Rods are more sensitive to movement and to low light. If you are appreciating the brush strokes on a Van Gough, you're using your cones. If you're battling 5 criminals in the glow of a distant street light (because everyone has a superhero fantasy) then it's mostly rods. Car racing is more of a rods than cones activity.

Novice racers tend to focus their eyes on objects close to their car. It almost seems if they can't see anything beyond the hood. Have you ever followed a car in a point-by session and waited an entire lap for them to notice you? You probably don't want to be that driver. Both on the track and on the street, your eyes should be up, looking ahead and scanning around you. If you focus too much attention on any one object, for example the car directly in front of you, you'll experience **tunnel vision** and you won't see the car right beside to you. Keeping your focus far ahead will free up your peripheral vision and allow you to multi-task better.

Your eyes are one of your most important tools to improving your lap times because vision is the primary means for picking out reference points. The key to getting faster is to continually experiment with the racing line. You should be asking yourself, "what if I turned in 5 feet earlier or touched the apex 3 feet deeper?" You can't answer these questions reliably without reference points. Exactly what is a reference point? Almost anything. Most commonly, it's the braking markers on the side of a track, but it could be tire tracks, a shrubbery, or a tree that becomes visible part way around a turn.

Reference points are also a way for drivers to communicate to each other how to drive a track. Simply stating, "I turn in when I feel like it" isn't nearly as useful to another driver as something like "I brake when my right tire hits the first apron, trail-brake around the next turn until the pavement changes color, and then aim for the flag stand. If I've nailed it, I'm at 5700 RPM when I leave the track out apron." Specific information tied to reference points is critical for consistency and for improving, and it starts with your eyes.

E is for Endurance Racing

Racing shouldn't be for rich idiots, but all idiots.

-- Jay Lamm

Budget endurance racing is a great way to get started in wheel-to-wheel racing. The cars are on the slow and cheap side which makes the racing on the safe and affordable side.

History

Budget endurance racing started out as a joke among a bunch of automotive journalists and enthusiasts back in 2005. The first series was called the "24 Hours of LeMons" and began in the San Francisco region in California, where foolhardy traditions often begin (the National Novel Writing Month is another example).

The main ideas behind *LeMons* runs counter-culture to enthusiast car culture. The cars are old, terrible, and mostly both. People dress up in silly costumes. The engineering is experimental to say the least. And the top prize of the race, the *Index of Effluency* goes to the car that somehow transcends its horribleness and runs for more laps than it should.

LeMons made amateur endurance racing surprisingly affordable and profitable. Getting an amateur road racing license with the SCCA, NASA, and other organizations can be a long and expensive process. Professional racing schools can set you back $10,000. Lemons doesn't require anything other than a driver's license. LeMons cars are also much cheaper. The public has responded by showing up in droves. At the 2014 race at Thunderhill, LeMons set a Guinness World Record for the largest road race in history with 216 on track at once!

Racing Series

Although the spirit of Lemons has remained mostly intact (they don't destroy one car per event anymore), other less subversive racing series have emerged. When 100+ cars routinely show up to a race, people are bound to notice... and copy. Today, there are several budget endurance racing series with similar enough rules that you can bring the same car and drivers to multiple series.

One of the charms of budget endurance racing is the wide range of cars, experience, and talent you find on track. When cool professionals, bewildered novices, and brazen amateurs share the same space... special things happen. Cars (and people) inevitably get bent out of shape, but more often than not, people leave smiling with memories they will treasure forever.

- **24 Hours of LeMons** is the original budget series and the one with the greatest sense of humor. Cars are supposed to cost $500 or less before safety equipment is added. You are allowed to sell off parts to mitigate costs. Cars are classified into classes A, B, or C depending on how competitive the car is, and penalty laps may be assessed in each class to equalize teams that appear to have advantages.

- **American Endurance Racing** has a full day of qualifying before the race that sets the class for car/team. Almost any production car is legal, and there are no rules governing costs. Drivers must have actual racing license or be veterans (5 races) of LeMons or the equivalent.

- **ChumpCar World Series** uses a point-based system to value the cars and their modifications in an effort to equalize performance and minimize cost. Cars that are over budget are given penalty laps.

- **Lucky Dog Racing League** classifies teams with 30 minutes of qualifying on the first race day. No experience necessary.

- **World Racing League** classifies by power:weight ratio using factory figures for power and scales for weight. Modifications to the car may see it bumped up a class. Previous track driving experience (HPDE) is required.

All of these racing organizations are serious about safety. You will need an SA approved helmet, SFI 38.1 neck protection, and fire retardant clothing (right down to your socks). Some of the safety rules are even more strict than what you would find in SCCA or NASA, especially when it comes to driving. Contact will automatically earn you a black flag which may include some penalty time and a driver swap. Generally, it doesn't matter who is the hitter and who is the hittee: everyone gets flagged.

Expenses

So exactly how cheap is budget racing? The typical endurance race is 12-16 hours with entry fees of $1000-$1200 for a 4-member team. There may be additional small fees for entering the property, camping, transponder rental, and annual dues. Each organization has its own pricing structure, but they all end up at about the same cost per hour.

Of course, in addition to event fees you have maintenance, repairs, consumables (fuel, tires, brake pads, etc.), travel, food, and housing. A race weekend can easily set you back $1000. But that value could be half or double depending on your specifics.

One way to offset expenses is by having arrive-n-drive guests who pay a rental fee to drive your car. Some people turn this into a business and make a little money, with the emphasis on little. Maintaining even a cheap race car can be expensive. One great way to experience budget endurance racing is to do an arrive-n-drive in someone else's car. Prices range from $500 to $2000 for the weekend, and you will probably have to sign a "you broke it, you pay for it" damage waiver.

Endurance Driving

The mentality of an endurance race is very different from a sprint race. In endurance races, the cars and drivers have to last hours. Driving the absolute limit the whole time causes excessive wear on the car and the driver. The best endurance teams set a pace they can keep lap after lap without getting into trouble. Most of the time, the team that wins the race doesn't record fast lap of the day. Drivers who are very aggressive usually end up wrecking the car and ruining the team's chance to win

F is for Flags

The best car safety device is a rear-view mirror with a cop in it.

-- Dudley Moore

Racing is controlled with a set of (almost) universal flags (**Figure F. 1**). The same flags are used from go-karting to Formula 1. Some of the most important flags are also the easiest to learn because the flags have the same color and general meaning as traffic light signals. But there are a lot more than just 3 flags.

▮	Stop	▮	Pit Now
▮	Go	◉	Mechanical Problem
▯	Caution	◰	Faster Cars Behind
▥	Hazard	▦	Session Over
▯	Safety Vehicle Ahead or Last Lap		

Figure F.1: Racing Flags

Flaggers

The job of a flagger is to keep you safe. Your first duty on track is to find the flaggers and make eye contact with them as you go around the track. Flaggers make subjective calls all the time, and having a good relationship with flaggers could save you from a black flag. You can't exactly strike up a conversation while going 3 wide through a corner, but acknowledging them with eye contact and nod of the head when the course is under caution is a good start. And behaving yourself in their corner isn't a bad idea either.

Red

Red means stop. Something bad has happened and everyone must park their car on the side of the track. Don't stop so quickly that you cause an accident behind you and don't stop in the middle of the track where you could get in the way of safety vehicles. If you can, stop before or after a hill because you could warp a rotor if you keep your brakes on for a prolonged period while they're hot. Stay in your car with the motor running (because it would be terribly embarrassing if you couldn't start it again). There's only one condition when you should get out of the car, and that's when it's on fire.

Green

Green means go. The race is on.

Yellow

Yellow means caution, and despite its brief appearance at traffic lights, it is the most common flag on a race track. Yellow is such an important flag that when pairs of flaggers work together, one flagger handles the yellow while the other flagger handles everything else. Once you see a yellow flag be prepared to **slow down**. Exactly how much to slow down is a judgement call. A waving yellow flag is more serious than a standing yellow flag. Slow down to about 1/2 speed if it's a waving flag. If it's a standing yellow at every station, cruise around at about 3/4 pace. But those are just rules of thumb. Be prepared to slow to a crawl, especially in a race with many cars.

The caution area generally starts perpendicular to the flag station waving the yellow flag, but racing up to the yellow flag is considered bad manners. **There is no passing under a yellow flag.** If you do, you will earn a black flag because it's both unsafe and unfair to pass under caution. Depending on your racing organization, there may be different protocols for when you are allowed to start racing again. You may be able to begin as soon as you pass the incident (e.g. stopped car), as soon as you can see a non-flagged corner station, or you may have to wait until you pass a non-flagged station. If you're unsure of the rules, wait until you pass a flag station without any flags.

Surface

Red & Yellow vertical stripes indicate there's something unusual about the road surface ahead. Common sources include dirt, oil, or car parts. Slow down to about 2/3 speed and tip-toe through the hazard, but be ready to go even slower. Wrecking the car when the flaggers have indicated a surface hazard is about the dumbest thing you can do.

White

A white flag has two interpretations. When shown at a flag station, it means there are safety vehicles ahead on track. Slow down and use caution when passing them. The safety vehicles themselves may also display a white flag. When shown at the start/finish line, it means there is one lap to go in the session. This can be very useful if you want to check tire temperatures and pressures. If you wait for the checkered flag, you might get stuck behind someone doing a slow cool-down lap.

Black

Black means bring your car into the pits. If all the flag stations are waving black flags, they need to clear the entire track. If they are waving the flag directly at you, you've done something wrong. In any case, if you see black, bring it in. It could be something as simple as having your window rolled up, or maybe you did something naughty like drove off track or hit another car. You need to leave the track immediately and talk to the race officials. Depending on the type of incident, they may simply send you right back out, or they may tell you you're done for the day.

Meatball

A black flag with an orange circle means your car is having a mechanical problem and you must leave the track. Drive to the track exit below racing speed and off the racing line. If you're leaking oil and you spread that all over the racing line, they will have to shut down the track for a while to clean it up. Nobody wants that.

Blue/Yellow

A blue flag with a diagonal stripe signals that there is a fast car approaching. It is waved at the slower car to give them a warning. That doesn't mean the driver in the slow car should pull over as if they were on the street with ambulances and fire trucks approaching. It is always the responsibility of the passing car to make a safe pass, but the slower car can make this much easier by driving a predictable line with a little less throttle and leaving some room on both sides of the car.

Checkered

The race/session is over. If you were in a test session and you want to take tire temperature and pressure readings, keep up your race pace and pit as quickly as you can. If you were racing, there's no reason to go fast. Slow down and enjoy the moment. That doesn't mean doing burnouts on track. Don't do that. You could get penalized by the racing organization and the track.

G is for Grip

We broke something, I think it was traction.

-- Carl Edwards

One doesn't usually think about gravity when it comes to racing, but it's pretty darn essential. Without gravity, tires would have no grip. This simple equation is the theoretical foundation.

The amount of grip (G) depends on the coefficient of friction of the tires (μ) and the weight of the vehicle (W). The weight of the vehicle at rest is simply its mass times the acceleration due to gravity. Downforce from wings and other aerodynamic features may increase weight while moving, but for now, let's assume the simple case that weight is due to gravity alone.

So grip is directly proportional to gravity. That is, if you double the weight, you double the grip. Except that it isn't so simple in reality (see "R is for Rubber"). The more grip you have, the faster you can go around a turn. Speed (V), grip (G), and corner radius (R) are related in the following equation.

We were first introduced to this equation back in "A is for Apex". At that time, we were concerned with how radius affects corner speed. Now let's turn our attention to grip. For any given corner, the more grip you have, the faster it's possible to go. You might say that grip equals speed. One of the simplest ways you can add speed to your car is to mount stickier tires.

Let's take a look at how 3 different tires perform in corners of varying radii. 0.8G is about what you can expect from a typical street tire. A tire meant for autocross or budget endurance racing will have about 1.0G of grip. An R-comp racing tire will have about 1.1G. These are very round figures and actual grip depends on the specific nature of the surface in addition to the weather. Don't get caught up in the absolute numbers here, it's the relative difference that matters.

Radius (ft)	0.8G (mph)	1.0G (mph)	1.1G (mph)
100	34.6	38.6	40.5
150	42.3	47.3	49.6
200	48.9	54.6	57.3
250	54.6	61.1	64.1
300	59.8	66.9	70.2
350	64.6	72.3	75.8
400	69.1	77.3	81.0
450	73.3	81.9	85.9
500	77.3	86.4	90.6

Imagine you're driving around a 300 ft radius turn on your favorite sport tires with 1.0G grip. Your maximum speed is about 66.9 mph. It's not possible to go faster than this no matter who the driver or what the car. However, a simple swap to R-comps would improve your corner speeds by about 5%. Is that a lot? No, it's a ton. Lap differences are often measured in tenths of a second. On a course with a 2 minute lap time, a 5% difference in speed is about 6 seconds.

Rain & Dirt

In the rain, your 1.0G tires will lose quite a bit of grip. When it first starts raining, it will be extra slippery because oils will be on the surface of the track. But after the oil washes away, the track will settle into something like 0.7G of grip. That's still plenty of grip for racing, but you will have to alter your racing line. The difference is more notable in acceleration than braking. A car that normally doesn't exhibit power on oversteer can suddenly feel like a drift machine. Watch out for that if your usual ride is a momentum car that never breaks traction under power.

Radius (ft)	Dry (mph)	Wet (mph)	Dirt (mph)
100	38.6	32.3	29.2
150	47.3	39.6	36.6
200	54.6	45.7	42.3
250	61.1	51.1	47.3
300	66.9	56.0	51.8
350	72.3	60.5	56.0
400	77.3	64.6	59.8
450	81.9	68.6	63.5
500	86.4	72.3	66.9

If you end up off track, traction is worse than if it was raining. Let's say you're in a 300 ft radius turn going 66 mph. You turn in too early and end up going wide at the exit with 2 wheels off track. Your 1.0G just plummeted to something like 0.6G. If your speed is 66 mph and your grip is 0.6G, your radius has to be around 500 ft minimum. If you keep your wheel wound up for a 300 ft radius, disaster is waiting.

Counter-steering

If your speed is too great for your radius, you have two options: (1) go off track while reciting the mantra "in a spin, to feet in" (2) open the wheel. That's right, there is an alternative! You can increase the radius of the turn by opening up the steering wheel. That is, if you were in a right-hand corner and you need to increase the radius, turn the wheel to the left. It's called counter-steering. It's surprising how many people in a panic situation do the exact opposite. When at the limit of adhesion, turning the wheel more doesn't turn the car more.

The best way to handle a too fast entry is by being pro-active about the recovery. Whether it's racing or life in general, it's better to meet trouble more than half way. As soon as you *suspect* you might be going off track, open the wheel to increase the radius and put 2 wheels of intentionally. If you keep the steering wheel cranked and hope that you will make it, two bad things can happen. (1) You may slide off track, spin, and wreck. (2) You might barely make it, which sends your brain a "phew, just made it" message. That's a far less useful thing to tell yourself than "handled it".

Off-track Excursions

Let's say you misjudged the entry speed and ended up having to open the wheel to avoid spinning. You're now a wheel or four off track and going mostly straight. Time to return to the racing surface. One of the common mistakes is turning the wheel too much. In the dirt, you have much less grip than normal, so the front wheels don't behave as if you're driving on asphalt, and the steering wheel will feel light in your hands. The knee-jerk response is to turn the steering wheel even more to get the damn car to turn. **Figure G.1** shows what can happen if you return to the track with too much steering lock.

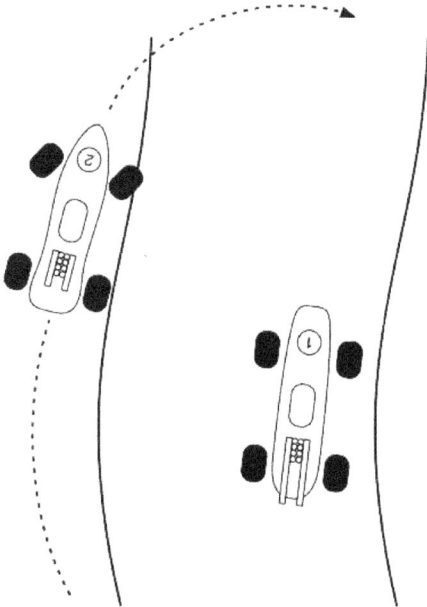

Figure G.1: Too Much Steering

When off track, the proper way to return is to ease the car back on with as little steering as possible. When your front tires get full grip, you want them pointed down the track in the direction the mass of the car is going.

Elevation

Changes in weight (and therefore grip) are most noticeable at the crest of a hill. Traction is lower, so there is a greater chance of running off track. Momentum cars that don't normally exhibit power oversteer/understeer can suddenly develop these characteristics. If there is any side-loading on the car and the wheels break free from too much power, the car will lose control. So don't hammer the throttle on the crest of a hill.

A downhill turn puts more weight on the front tires than rear, so the car will be prone to oversteer. Lifting off throttle in a downhill turn can snap the back around. If you're approaching a downhill turn, it's much better to get rid of your speed before the turn because it's dangerous to do it in the turn.

An uphill turn puts more weight on the rear tires. Your front tires will have less traction and you may find yourself wondering why the steering wheel doesn't do anything. Slowing down will add traction and restore steering.

Camber

NASCAR oval tracks are all on-camber. Drivers hardly appear to turn the wheel because the track does some of the turning for them. On-camber turns can therefore be taken faster because their radii are effectively larger. On camber turns also add extra load to the tires which increase their grip. The net effect is that on-camber turns are bigger and grippier than they appear. Have fun with that.

Off-camber turns present a difficult problem. Novices hate them but experienced drivers love them for the challenge they present. Off-camber turns push you away from the apex, and therefore require more steering lock than you expect. This makes the turn radius effectively tighter. They also unweight the car in the wrong direction, decreasing the load on the car and consequently the available grip. It's as if someone suddenly threw sand under your car. Have even more fun with that.

If you have a choice about which line to take through a corner, maximize the use of on-camber and minimize the use of off-camber.

H is for Heel-Toe

It doesn't matter what gear you're in when you hit the wall.

--Duck Waddle

Today, heel-toe shifting is generally taught as an advanced driving technique, but it used to be the standard way to downshift a car. This is one of those racing skills you are actually encouraged to practice in your street car. Not only does it give you lots of practice time, it also increases the lifespan of your transmission components.

Pedal Setup

Heel-toe shifting is much easier if your pedals are set up correctly. The brake and throttle should be close enough to each other so that your foot can press both simultaneously without turning your foot right or left. This is shown in panel **A** in **Figure H.1**. When you press the brake all the way down, it should be a tiny bit higher than the throttle. The heel should be anchored on the floor to provide control. The ball of your right foot will be on the the brake pedal and the right half of your foot will be free. By rotating at the ankle, you should be able to press the throttle with the outside of your foot.

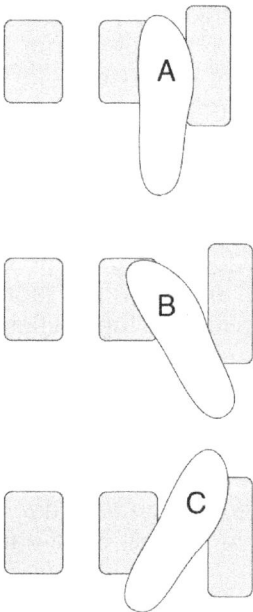

Figure H.1: Feet & Pedals

If your pedals are set up too wide or the throttle is too high, you have to change your foot geometry. Panel **B** shows the technique of having the ball of your foot on the brake and the heel pressing the throttle. The main disadvantage of this is that your heel must leave the floor. Your braking sensitivity will be much greater if you keep your heel planted. Panel **C** shows heel on brake and toe on throttle. Not only do you have to remove your heel from the floor, you have to actuate the brake with a part of your foot that has very little control. It's not recommended, but if the ergonomics of your car prevent you from moving your knee inward as in panel **B**, there isn't much you can do about it.

Heel-Toe Technique

The best way to downshift is using heel-toe technique, which is also called a **blip-shift**. This requires your right foot to be able to actuate both the brake and throttle *at the same time*. You'll find several variations of the technique and some very long-winded descriptions. I'm going to make it much simpler: move both feet in unison. When the right foot is on the throttle, the left foot is on the dead pedal. When the right foot is on the brake (and partially throttle), the left foot is on the clutch. Here's the sequence of events.

1. Move feet from outside pedals to inside pedals
2. Keep braking, and blip the throttle at the end of the braking zone
3. Downshift
4. Move feet from inside pedals to outside pedals

Don't blip or downshift until the very end of the braking zone. If you blip too soon, you may over-rev the engine.

Clutch-less shifting and double-clutching

Imagine you're in the most important endurance race in your life and your clutch has just given up. You could drive the rest of the race in whatever gear you happen to be in, or you could shift without the clutch. It turns out to be pretty simple to upshift without a clutch. If you ease off the throttle, the shifter will come out of gear with a gentle nudge. It will also go into a higher gear with a gentle nudge as the revs fall to the point where the engine, transmission, and wheels get into sync. Downshifting is less difficult than you might imagine. You just have to get the transmission spinning faster. To do this, put the car in neutral with your left foot off the clutch. Now blip the throttle and the transmission will speed up. If you press the shifter into the lower gear at the right moment, it will click into place. If it grinds and pops back out, you missed it. Spin it up with another blip and try again.

Double-clutching or more properly double-declutch downshifting is a heel-toe technique in which you blip from neutral with the clutch engaged.

1. Move right foot from throttle to brake
2. Press the clutch in (#1), shift to neutral, release clutch
3. Blip the throttle while still braking (of course)
4. Press the clutch in (#2), shift to lower gear, release clutch
5. Move right foot from brake to throttle

In general, it's better to blip from neutral with the clutch engaged. This spins up both the transmission and the engine rather than just the engine. If you blip with the clutch pedal down, you're spinning up just the engine, and the synchronizer gear will take more wear when you shift. This is why double clutching is preferred.

Blip After Braking

If you're driving a car that has poorly placed pedals, you might not be able to heel-toe. You can still rev match, but you can't brake and blip at the same time. Complete your braking and then blip before you shift. Again, it's best to blip from neutral with the clutch engaged.

Slipping the Clutch

Slipping the clutch is not good for the clutch, but it's better to slip the clutch than get into an accident. So if you can't match revs, you'll have to engage the clutch slowly. If you *dump the clutch*, you may lock up your wheels, which could cause sudden oversteer (RWD) or understeer (FWD).

Some drivers are very fast without matching revs. They put more wear on their car, but the clutch is a relatively inexpensive part (although it can be a lot of labor).

I is for Insurance

Fun is like life insurance; the older you get, the more it costs.

-- Kin Hubbard

High performance driver education events (HPDE) are a great way to practice track driving in a street-legal car. But do you know what will happen if you crash your car at the race track? Apart from your family shaking their head at you that is. Will your insurance cover you? Some companies do, but most do not. The more it appears as if you were racing, the more likely you'll be denied coverage. Do you have a sports car? Do you have racey bits on your car? Do you have a lap timer? Were you being timed? Did the organization have *racing* or *speed* in its title?

Before you head to the track, you should find out what your insurance policies cover. It may make you think twice about driving your brand new sports car at high speed.

Just Walk Away

Crashing an expensive car on track can be terribly painful financially and emotionally. The simplest way to avoid this is to bring a cheap car you don't care about. It's much easier to walk away from a 1990s Miata than a brand new Porsche Cayman S. There's an old saying that if you can't afford to push your car off a cliff at the end of the day, don't bring it to the track. Believe it or not, you can have just as much fun in an old beater as the latest supercar. You might even have more fun with a car you're not afraid to drive beyond the limit.

It is more fun to drive a slow car fast than to drive a fast car slow.

-- Abner Perney

Track Day Insurance

If you really want to bring your expensive car to the track and experience it in all its glory, you ought to protect yourself with supplemental insurance that is specifically tailored to track driving. In the USA, there is Lockton Motorsports. Canada has Track Day Insurance Canada. Europe has insuremytrackday.com. There are surely other companies as well. Use your Google skills and comparison shop. You can purchase single days or long term contracts. The rates are surprisingly affordable. For single days, the price is similar to what you pay for track fees. The rates go down, of course, if you purchase several days at once or sign up for a long term contract. Insurance can give you the peace of mind to fully enjoy your track day, and you'll probably drive better too.

Insurance Fraud

Crashing your car on track and then claiming it happened on the street is a form of insurance fraud. Penalties range from fines to prison sentences.

J is for Judgement

Newmans' first law: It's useless to put on your brakes when you're upside down.

-- Paul Newman

You can give people a list of things they are supposed to do, but bad consequences are often a better teacher. One way to appreciate the horror stories of racing is to search YouTube for racing crashes. You'll see spins, fires, crashes into walls, destroyed cars, and impacts so hard you will wonder if the driver died. Amateur racing is relatively safe because the speeds are low and the safety requirements are high, but hitting a wall at 100 mph is still hitting a wall at 100 mph. You might not die, but your car will be scrap metal and you might be walking with a limp for a year.

I write a blog called "You suck at racing: a crash course in auto racing". Every week features a brief analysis of a racing incident from some form of amateur car race. Check out the blog, but you should also do your own YouTube crash research, especially at your favorite track. It will show specific areas where people get into trouble. If your track is also on iRacing or some other simulator, go online and watch where people wreck. It will be in the same place.

This is amateur racing. There's no professional racing contract in your future. If you're about to enter your first race, the best advice I can give you is to imagine you are racing *with* others not *against* them. Share the track, share the enjoyment, and if it comes to it, take more than your fair share of the blame.

Don't Speed in the Paddock

The first place you can get into trouble at the track isn't even on the track. Driving around the paddock too fast endangers people, cars, dogs, and property. Track stewards may penalize you and if you do something really egregious (e.g. donuts and burnouts), they may fine you and/or kick you off the property.

Obey the Blend Line

When you enter the track, there is generally a **blend line** painted on the surface (**Figure J.1**). You're not supposed to cross this line when you enter the track. Stay on the outside of the track until you are completely clear of the blend line. Then, and only then, should you consider moving onto the racing line.

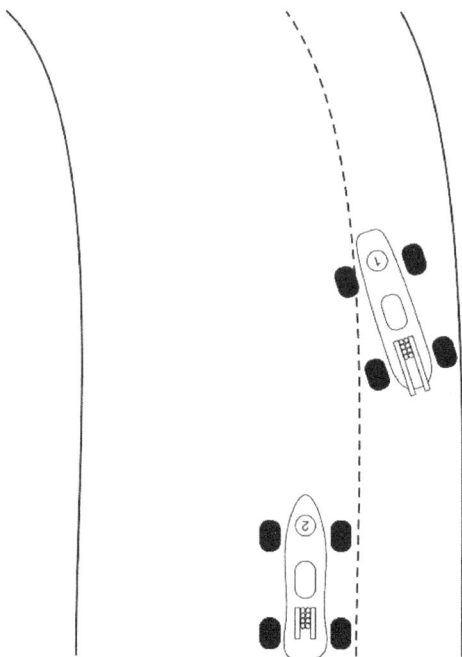

Figure J.1: The Blend Line

Just like when merging onto the highway, you shouldn't change lanes until you are up to speed and the lane is clear. Turning in too quickly could cause faster cars to hit you. Ignoring the blend line is a good way to earn a black flag.

Drive the Racing Line on Practice Days

At a track day in which the cars are not racing, it is safest to drive the racing line at all times. That generally means slow in, fast out, late apex, large radius. Faster cars behind you will expect you to take this line. When they want to get around you, it's their responsibility to go off the racing line and pass you where it is safe for them to do so (usually on a straight). You can make it easier for them by slowing down a little and giving them a point-by. Driving off line may put you in an unfamiliar part of the track with one hand out your window, 2 wheels in the dirt, and your car spinning across track. So drive predictably and safely by staying on the line. On race day, however, robotically driving the racing line could get you into heaps of trouble.

Don't Steal Apexes

One of the most common accidents is caused by the dive-bomb (**Figure J.2**). A faster car decides to pass a slower car on the inside of a corner. If the faster car is much faster, this often works out okay. But *often* isn't nearly safe enough. If the lead car has turned into the corner, it *owns* the corner and has every right to the apex. Stealing the apex isn't just rude, it's dangerous.

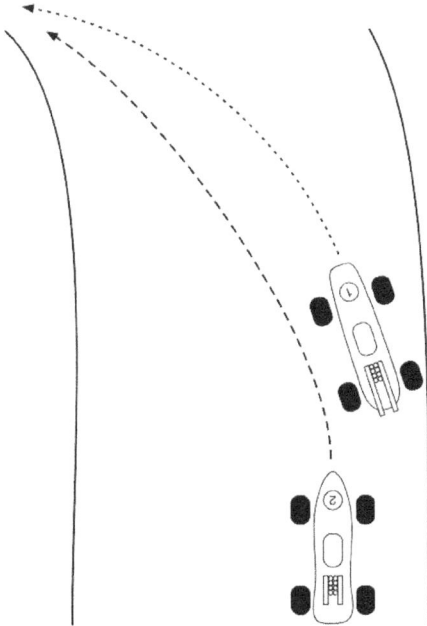

Figure J.2: Dive-bombing

If you're in the faster car, do you really want to take the chance that the slower car is going to make room for you? Or that the slower car even sees you? Don't take that chance. You have a faster car, so you're going to pass it anyway. Take your time. The alternative sounds like "screeeeeee krunch".

Don't Steal Entries

Novice drivers have a habit of robotically driving the racing line even at low speeds. If you're approaching a slow driver, expect them to set up on the outside of the track without checking their mirrors. If you sneak up along side them on the outside, you may find them accidentally side-swiping you (**Figure J.3**) as they set up for the corner entry.

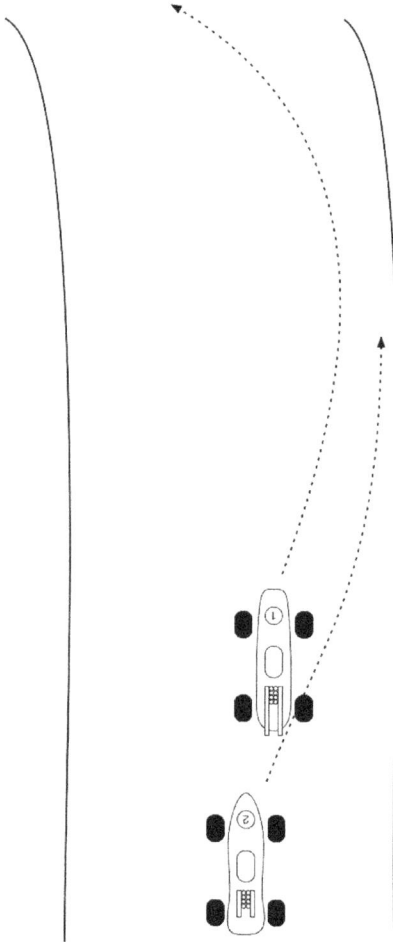

Figure J.3: Side-swipe

Don't Steal Exits

In a race with mixed cars or mixed abilities, some of the cars may be annoyingly off pace. You may find yourself quite suddenly on the bumper of one of these cars in the middle of a corner. Due to your fast closing speed, they may not see you, especially if their attention is on the apex. You can't expect these cars to make room for you. It's their corner. And even if you can put yourself into position to have right of way, rules don't prevent accidents: you do. Give the slow driver the space to track out or drive badly. You'll be past them soon enough. The alternative may find you getting pinched at the exit (**Figure J.4**).

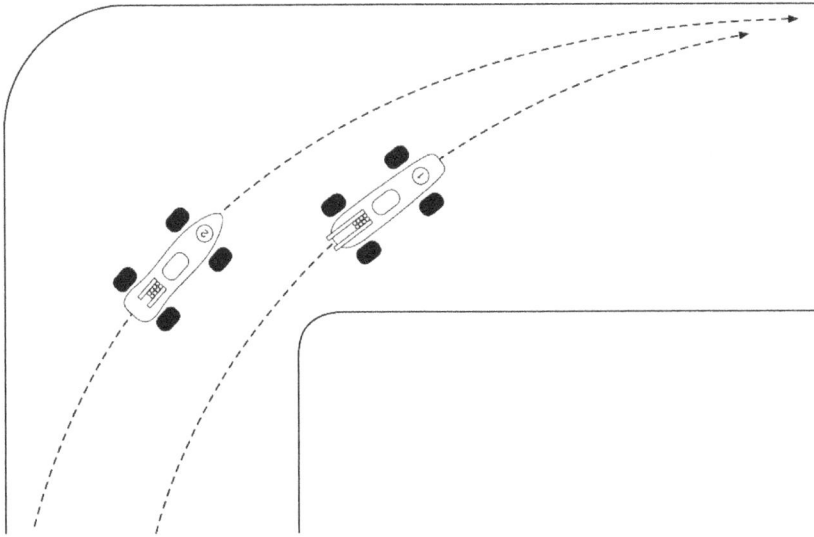

Figure J.4: Pinched at the Exit

Drive Defensively

A lot of accidents can be prevented by driving defensively. Assume the other drivers don't see you. Check your mirrors often and drive the safest line rather than the fastest line. If you're approaching a corner and you see a car behind you maneuver to steal your apex, stick your car in front of them and drive around the inside of the corner. Closing the door on them should prevent them from dive-bombing you, but if they are reckless and you get hit, at least you'll take the impact on your bumper, not a wheel.

Note that you can drive too defensively. If you drive so defensively that you become unpredictable, you will be a hazard to everyone around you.

Slow Down for Incidents

If a car spins or goes off track in front of you, slow down. The competitor in you might want to take advantage of their misfortune and speed by, but you risk getting hit by the car as it changes direction suddenly. If you do get hit, it's much better to take the impact on the front bumper. So aim your car at them as you slow down.

Don't Drive Beyond Your Limit

It's easy to tell someone not to drive beyond their limit, but lots of novices don't even know their limit. Add to that the excitement of racing, and it's easy to misjudge one's own abilities. Ultimately, it's up to you to drive responsibly and within your limit. When in doubt, drive slower, especially going into a corner.

K is for Kit

Auto racing, bull fighting, and mountain climbing are the only real sports... all others are just games.

-- Ernest Hemingway

Safety starts with your personal safety equipment. Don't buy the cheapest thing you find used or online. You'll end up replacing it and paying more in the end. Borrowing or renting is better than buying cheap.

Head & Neck

Cars and motorcycles have slightly different considerations and safety ratings (SA for cars, DOT for motorcycles). You need an SA rated helmet for auto racing with a sticker less than 10 years old. A full-face helmet will protect you from grinding/burning your face off in the event of a catastrophe, so get one of those and not an open face. Every head is shaped a little differently, so it's a good idea to shop for one in person rather than buying online.

One of the most important safety items in your kit is an SFI 38.1 compliant neck brace. The original HANS device is the most popular, but products are now available from multiple vendors including Necksgen, Leatt, Simpson, and Z-Tech. These neck braces prevent your head from separating from your neck in a violent deceleration. That's called a **basilar skull fracture** and it has accounted for the deaths of numerous famous race drivers. All professional drivers wear 38.1 neck braces now and amateur racing organizations are starting to follow suit. In order to use a 38.1 neck brace, your car needs a roll cage, roll bar, or harness bar to strap into. It's not a great idea to drive on track without these. If you can't strap your 38.1 device into a harness, considering getting a Simpson Hybrid, which attaches the neck restraint to your body.

Figure K.1: Necksgen

Figure K.2: Z-Tech

Fire Retardant Clothing

In order to give you the best chance of surviving a fire, all of your clothing should be made from Nomex or other fire retardant fabric. On practice days you might not be required to wear full Nomex gear, but on a race day you will. You can either wear a heavy, triple layered suit, or a lighter suit plus full Nomex underwear. The racing suit, gloves, and shoes need to be stamped with SFI labels. Even if you happen to have fire fighting gear that exceeds racing standards, it needs an SFI label or they won't allow you on track. You also need Nomex socks and balaclava (head sock) though these don't usually carry SFI stickers.

Cooling

On a hot day, you can spend more mental energy dealing with discomfort than driving. That can decrease performance and increase risk. A really good way to keep cool is a liquid cooled shirt. F.A.S.T. and Coolshirt Systems are two popular brands. Cold water is circulated from an ice chest through a shirt with flexible hosing sewn into it. If you're clever, you can build your own system with an ice chest, bilge pump, and vinyl tubing. It's even possible to sew aquarium tubing into a shirt. The professionally-built systems are not that expensive and as they are safety equipment, so your thought should be safety first.

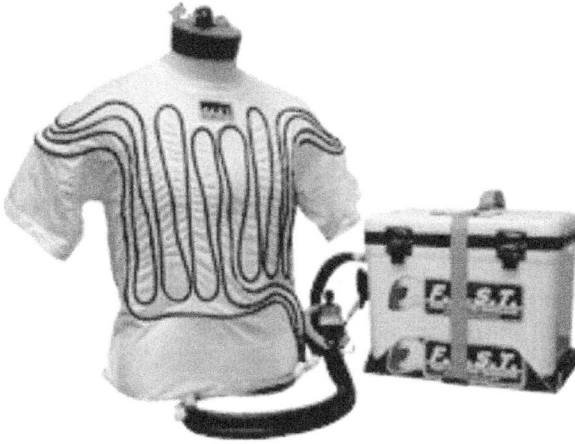

Figure K.3: F.A.S.T. cooling system

A less complicated alternative is a StaCool vest. These have pockets that are filled with removable cold packs. Beware of vests with phase-change materials. Although they have the advantage of staying at a constant temperature, some are flammable, toxic, or both.

Figure K.4: StaCool Vest

Drinking

Hydrating yourself is easy enough to do. Install a drinking system in your car. This can be as simple as a backpacking unit with the hose dangling within reach.

Dehydration is a serious concern on the race track. Once you become **hypohydrated**, you body no longer performs optimally. Not only will this affect your lap times, it increases your risk of accidents. You start to feel the effects of dehydration when your body loses about 1% body weight. For a 200 lb driver, that's 2 pounds, or 32 oz of water. You might think that all your weight loss is from sweating, but a surprising amount is lost through breathing. So you can be dehydrated without looking like it, especially in a dry climate. You can easily lose 5 pounds driving for 2 hours on a hot day in full racing gear.

Hypohydration reduces your blood volume, decreases blood flow in your skin, decreases sweating, and interferes with your cooling. As a result, your core body temperature will increase, which affects both physical and mental abilities. Dehydration is bad enough, but coupled with overheating is really dangerous. It's difficult to detect that your body is underperforming, but the drop in performance and the inability to detect are well documented.

Diapers

Needing to urinate while on track is uncomfortable and distracting. Adult diapers are the answer. You might feel silly wearing them at first, but cutting your stint down by an hour because you don't want to relieve yourself in the car is far sillier.

L is for Library

It is unlikely that you will ever get to sit down and have a one on one discussion on the driving of the racing car with the likes of Jackie Stewart, Emerson Fittipaldi, Niki Lauda and Alain Prost. But you can sure as hell read what they have to say about it.

-- Carroll Smith

Unlike basketball, where you can practice shooting for hours every day for free, practice time in racing is much more expensive and precious. To make the most of your on-track time, you have to do as much off-track homework as your schedule allows. You can learn a surprising amount about the theory of driving from books and videos. Your **library** is your theoretical foundation. Once you mix that with your practical skills (see "M is for Muscle Memory") you'll see great improvement.

Essential Reading

There are several really good books on racing written by world-renown authorities on the subject. Read as many as you can. There's really no downside to building your knowledge base.

- If you buy just one book, make it "Ultimate Speed Secrets" by Ross Bentley. If you buy just two, buy a second copy of the same book and give it to a friend. Ross takes a very thoughtful, logical, and practical approach to driving. The writing is simple, direct, and easily digested. Yet the content is deep and you will find something to appreciate every time you re-read it. The *Ultimate* book collects most of what are in his other books, but if you're a driving nerd, you may want all of them. Ross is very active in driver education, and I highly recommend subscribing to his weekly newsletter and YouTube channel. Also, if you get a chance, attend one of his seminars or webinars. He's an engaging speaker.

- "Driving to Win" by Carroll Smith is brutally frank about the demands of racing, and to those not up to the task, he often employs the phrase *other sports beckon*. This short phrase is an indication of his personality, which may endear him to some readers and turn off others. He's a little old-fashioned, so prepare to roll your eyes the occasional male chauvinism. In addition to all the tips on driving, there's a lot of information about what it takes to become a professional. Smith is equally famous for his other "To Win" books on racecar engineering and tuning. Most of the serious racers have them all.

- "Going Faster! Mastering the Art of Race Driving" by the Carl Lopez of the Skip Barber Racing School is the racing bible for many drivers. One reason for that is the school is one of the largest in the world, having homes at more than 20 tracks. The book is comprehensive, up-to-date, and well written, but lacks some of the personality of the two books above. If you're serious about driving, it belongs on your bookshelf and on your Summer reading list every year.

Primers

Less intimidating to the novice, the following books are short but great. Pick them up used and give them to friends.

- "You Suck at Racing": Oh wait, that's the book you're reading.

- "The Ace Factor: a guide to what you need to know about vintage racing", by E. Paul Dickinson, is 65 pages of wonderfully succinct instruction. It's nearly the perfect beginner's guide to auto racing (there's only a few sentences about vintage racing). It's included free with some vintage racing membership packages and still in print.

- "Sports Car and Competition Driving" by Paul Frère is a complete resource for the beginning driver. Not only does it describe the usual basics of cornering, car dynamics and setup, it backs that up with a little of the physics behind the scenes. It also has sections on training, weather, front-wheel drive, and a bunch of do's and don'ts. In 1963, when it was first published, it must have been the ideal first book. Although it was updated in 1992, it feels a little old.

Supplemental Reading

- "Think Fast: the Racer's Why-To Guide to Winning" by Neil Roberts blends very practical advice with theoretical considerations. This is an excellent introduction to the physics of racing. Even though it is written by an engineer, the author recognizes that there's more tuning in the driver than the car. Highly recommended for the more cerebral drivers.

- "Race to Win" by Derek Daly has a lot of practical advice for the aspiring professional driver. Unlike most books on driving, this one has almost nothing to do with driving. Instead, it focuses on the support structure around the driver, which may be even more critical to success than the driver or car. Auto racing is such an expensive and stressful sport that the team around the driver has an unusually important role. The content transcends auto racing to all walks of life and could equally well be a book on proper parenting.

- "Competition Driving" by Alain Prost and Pierre-Francois Rousselot explains the basics well and has some excellent advice from Prost sprinkled throughout. It's not many pages, and the color photos, glossy paper, fonts, and layout give it the appearance it was designed for children. But don't judge a book by its cover, it's a serious work. You can pick it up pretty cheap used.

- "Driving in Competition" by Alan Johnson is famous because it introduced the 3 kinds of corners: slow-in-fast-out, fast-in-slow-out, and compromises. While interesting from a historical perspective, it's a little dated. It is also somehow both too brief and too wordy.

- "The Racing Driver" by Denis Jenkinson is an interesting piece of racing journalism. Jenkinson was one of the most successful *passengers* in motorsport both in cars and sidecars. He may be most famous for codifying the tenths system. Interestingly, he has been misinterpreted by almost everyone. He suggested that most racing was performed at 8 tenths. 9.5 tenths was something that happened occasionally during a race, but every moment at 10 tenths was a disaster waiting to happen. Unlike Spinal Tap, he did not go to 11.

- "The Physics of Racing" by Brian Beckman is a series of articles written over more than 10 years that uses back of the envelope calculations to introduce and solve various aspects of racecar driving and engineering. This series is an excellent introduction to the math behind speed. You can find the series at several sites. Here's one http://phors.locost7.info/contents.htm

- "Fast Car Physics" by Chuck Edmonson is less approachable than The Physics of Racing, but has much greater depth. If you're an engineer who wants *all* the details, this is your book.

- "Going Nowhere Fast In Assetto Corsa: Race Driving On A Simulator" by Amen Zwa is a comprehensive guide to simracing from hardware to software to user. Zwa is an engineer, and it shows in his writing. His book is meticulously organized with great attention to detail. It focuses on Assetto Corsa, which was released in late 2014. If you've never done any simracing, Assetto Corsa is probably as good a place to start as any.

- The "Becoming an Alien" series by iRacer X includes titles on "Unlocking the Secret of Speed", "Mastering the Art of Braking", "Learning to Drift (and Going Faster)", and "How to Overtake, Defend, and Win". These are short Kindle books at $0.99 each and while they are targeted at the iRacing simulation community, the content applies equally to real driving.

YouTube

YouTube is an excellent resource for driving videos. It's a lot easier to learn from other drivers when you have intimate knowledge of a track. So look for videos of your home track, not just any track. Also, look for videos of people who drive similar cars at similar speeds. If the car or driver is too different, it's more difficult to see what you're doing better or worse.

There are typically 3 kinds of good videos: (1) turn-by-turn guides (2) races (3) spins, crashes, and other incidents. There are some excellent turn-by-turn track walkthroughs that will help you find the typical racing line. But the track-day line is a best case scenario, so watch races also to see what people do when they are door to door. Spins and wrecks can help you remember what not to do and where not to do it. The more violent the crash, the more it cements the lesson into your brain. Visit my blog at yousuckatracing.wordpress.com for a weekly crash video and analysis.

Forums

You can find a lot of great driving advice on various online racing forums. Find one and start becoming a member of an online community. It's a good way to learn, teach, and make new friends. Forum posts often link to other resources, so they are an excellent way to keep up on the latest racing technology, such as which tire is best this year. Ignore the abrasive personalities you may encounter. There are valuable ways to spend your off-track time and arguing with people who want to be argued with is not one of them.

Magazines

Magazines tend to focus on the latest in car technology. Amateur racing tends to be done with older cars. As such, magazines aren't the best resources for amateur racing. One exception is Grassroots Motorsports, which routinely has articles on racing and preparing cheap cars.

M is for Muscle Memory

Suddenly I realized that I was no longer driving the car consciously. I was driving it by a kind of instinct, only I was in a different dimension.

-- Ayrton Senna

You can probably ride a bike. But can you ride no-handed? While spinning plates in both hands? And one on your head? Can you drop into a half pipe and do 720° on the opposite side? Probably not. Riding a bike around town is not like riding a bike in a circus or a half pipe. And driving a car around town is not like driving a car around a race track.

How does a circus performer or X-games biker ride with such skill? Not by thinking about it. Their nervous systems are hard-wired from thousands of hours of training to perform autonomously. It would be suicidal for you to try to back-flip a motorcycle if all you've ever done is grocery runs. But if you've practiced for years the risk would be minimal. So what makes you think you can safely race a car without putting in your hours?

4 Stages of Competence

Before I learned the art, a punch was just a punch, and a kick, just a kick. After I learned the art, a punch was no longer a punch, a kick, no longer a kick. Now that I understand the art, a punch is just a punch and a kick is just a kick.

-- Bruce Lee

The *conscious competence* model for learning new skills breaks down competence into 4 categories.

1. **Unconscious incompetence** - I don't know what I don't know

2. **Conscious incompetence** - I recognize how little I know

3. **Conscious competence** - I perform best when I concentrate

4. **Unconscious competence** - I perform best when I don't concentrate

By the simple act of grabbing this book, you have already begun to get past the first stage. Reading and watching will help you through the second stage and give you a theoretical foundation for the third. But learning how to *do* something will take more than reading. In order to be safe on track, you need to get to the fourth stage where your body acts without thinking. That's entirely on you putting your hours in.

Self-education is, I firmly believe, the only kind of education there is.

-— Isaac Asimov

Like any sport, racing takes a great deal of training. Have you ever reached par on 36 holes, bowled a 300, or scored 25 in a round of skeet? Some people train a lifetime and never reach such goals. But this is the realm of talented amateurs. Professionals are even better. In Malcom Gladwell's popular work "Outliers: The Story of Success", he explains that the key to attaining world-class expertise is 10,000 hours of training. That's a 40 hour work week for 5 years. Unless you're incredibly wealthy, it's hard to spend that kind of time on a race track.

So let's forget about you and I becoming professional racers for the moment and focus on something more important: survival. In order to be safe in a wheel to wheel race, you need the forethought to avoid dangerous situations, the muscle memory to control a sliding car, and the experience to make the right decision. These thoughts and actions must be automatic. There's no way to learn these skills from a book. They are developed from hundreds if not thousands of hours of training. If this is starting to sound repetitive, so is training.

Sliding

The biggest difference between street and track driving is that your tires don't slide on the street and they slide constantly on track. A car sliding its tires on the street is out of control and possibly breaking the law. A car not sliding its tires on track is being driven under the limit. Racecars do not "corner like they are on rails". How a car behaves while sliding is much more important that how it behaves under the limit. A sliding car feels somewhat like downhill skiing, snowboarding, water skiing, ice skating, surfing etc. But in these sports, there's no way not to slip, so sliding feels normal. You must get to the point where sliding your car feels completely normal and you can control it without conscious thought.

When I say *sliding* I don't mean *drifting*. Drifting looks awesome and takes a great deal of skill. Every racing driver should practice some drifting because it improves oversteer recovery. But drifting is not the fast way around a race track because the rear tires are losing traction from over-spinning and the front tires are not slipping at all. The fastest way around a track is in a mild 4-wheel slide.

N is for Nadir

Oh yes. It's not when you brake but when you take them off that counts. Most people don't understand that.

-- Jackie Stewart

Instructors and their novice students generally focus on hitting the entry, apex, and exit of every corner, and this is a good driving exercise to learn a track. But *hitting your spots* doesn't necessarily reduce lap times (or make you safer). You have to hit these spots at the correct speed and correct angle. It's relatively easy to play connect the dots through a corner at low speed. Doing it at full speed in a 4-wheel drift is something else entirely.

The word *apex* means top. If every corner has a top, then every corner ought to have a bottom too. Let's call that its *nadir*, and define it as the point of minimum speed. This generally occurs as your foot is making the transition from brake to throttle. In **Figure N. 1**, the box shows the position of the nadir in a typical 90° corner.

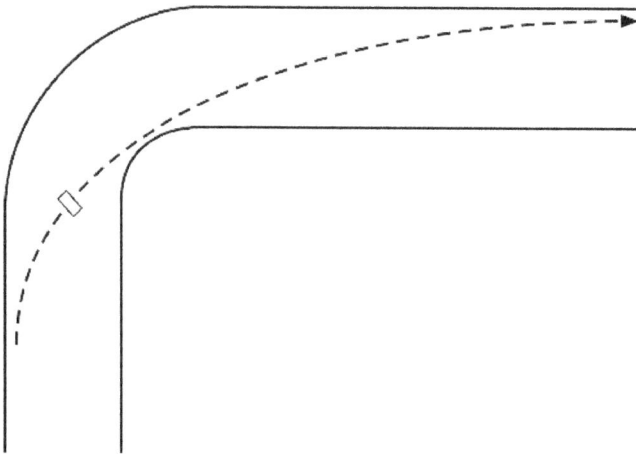

Figure N.1: The Nadir

Most people talk about the entry, apex, and track out, but it's much more informative to talk about the nadir. It's not always possible (or even desirable) to be on the optimal racing line in every corner. Traffic in front and behind dictates what kind of line you can take. Instead of focusing on three points, try focusing on just the nadir because it simplifies your goal: get to the nadir, get away from nadir.

Position & Angle

Where exactly is the nadir of a corner? As a general rule, in a Type 1 corner, the nadir is before the apex. In a Type 2 corner, it is after the apex. The nadir depends on the racing line, but for any given racing line, there will be a point of minimum speed. If you arrive there with too much speed, you can't stay on the line, which means you may run off track. If you arrive there with too little speed, your mid-corner and exit speeds will suffer.

The nadir also has an angle. Two drivers can have the same minimum speed at the same position of the track but their cars can be pointed in slightly different directions. While it is easy to plot speed and position with almost any telemetry device, the angle is not so easy, and therefore hard to analyze. The optimal angle depends on many factors from the interaction of the tires with the surface, to the balance and power of the car.

The most important thing to realize about the nadir is that it cannot be optimized with courage, aggression, or luck. The nadir has an exact speed, location, and angle. You can't bully it into submission anymore than you can trick it into compliance. It takes precision and practice.

The Approach

Since the nadir of the corner is the slowest part, it follows that everything that happens before the nadir involves your car slowing down. This may be threshold braking, scrubbing speed with your tires, trail-braking, or just lifting off the throttle. Your braking and speed estimation skills are critical. Although some time can be gained by getting to the nadir as quickly as possible, your emphasis should be on arriving at the precise optimal speed so you can get away with the greatest speed.

Too Fast

What happens if you arrive at the nadir too fast? In **Figure N.2**, path **A** is the optimal line and path **B** shows what happens when you have too much speed at the nadir. There's simply no way you can stay on the **A** line anymore. You have to open the wheel, increase the radius of the turn, pick a new nadir, and delay application of the throttle. It's not that big a deal if you miss your favorite nadir. Just find a new one. Overcooking the entry happens all the time in racing, especially when being aggressive.

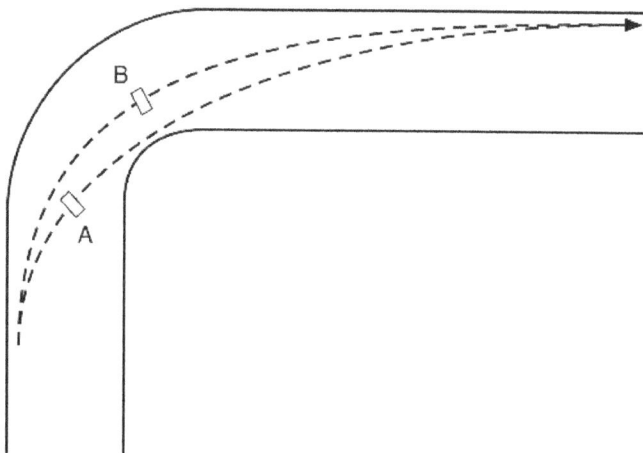

Figure N.2: Too Fast at the Nadir

Too Slow

Figure N.3 shows what can happen if you enter too slow. Path **A** shows an early switch from brakes to throttle. At this point if you add the typical amount of throttle you'll be going too fast. The radius of the turn will have to increase to compensate, and you will miss the apex and run out of room at the exit. Not good. To save yourself from going off track, you may have to go off throttle a second time. It's very messy and slow.

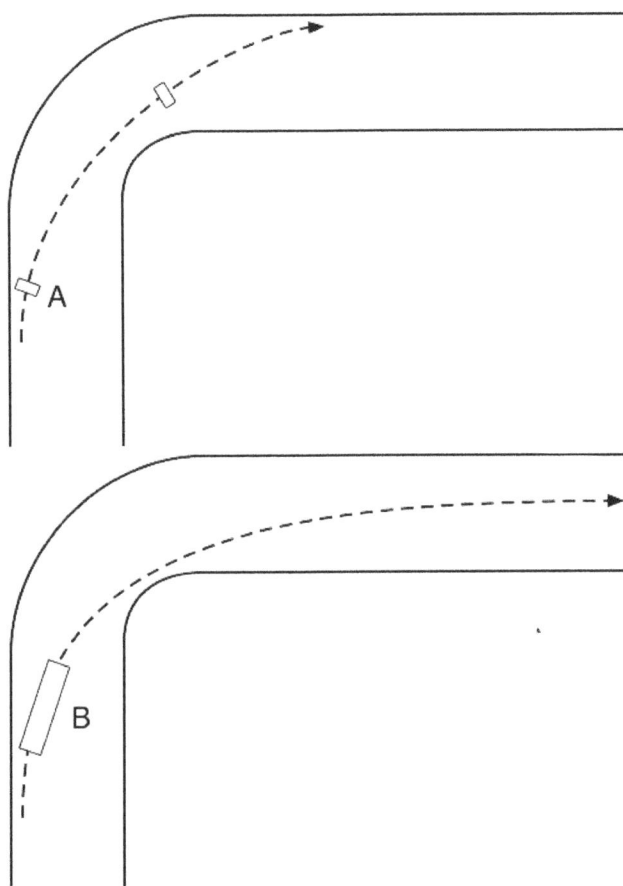

Figure N.3: Too Slow at the Nadir

The better way to handle a too slow entry is to accept your mistake, not try to make up for it (path **B**). Coast until you get to the usual place you add throttle. Since you're down on speed, your tires have excess grip for the usual line. You can therefore retain a little steering lock and shorten the track. Once you've blown the entry and mid-corner, there's really no point in tracking all the way out. It just makes the track longer. So the nadir is in the same position, but the angle changes to reflect the increased grip.

The Departure

Everything after the nadir should involve your car speeding up. If you have to release the throttle or add steering you messed up. You should be increasing throttle and unwinding steering. Some corners may require a very gradual increase in throttle as you balance cornering and accelerating forces. This is especially true in vehicles with lots of power or when faced with adverse camber or a cresting turn.

Corners Revisited

Back in "C is for Corners" we looked at the racing line through isolated an combined corners. Let's revisit that a little thinking about the nadir. **Figures N.4, N.5, and N.6** show the position of the nadir on 180° turns with an increasing amount of straight between them.

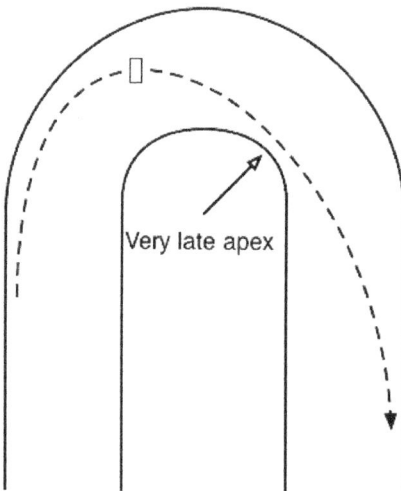

Very late apex

Figure N.4: Hairpin Nadir

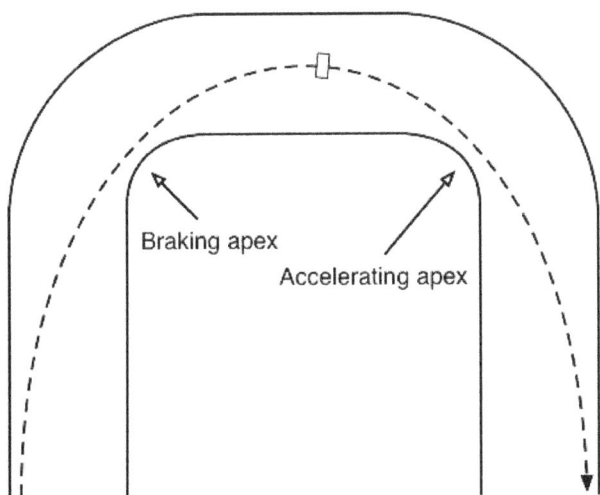

Figure N.5: Double Apex Nadir

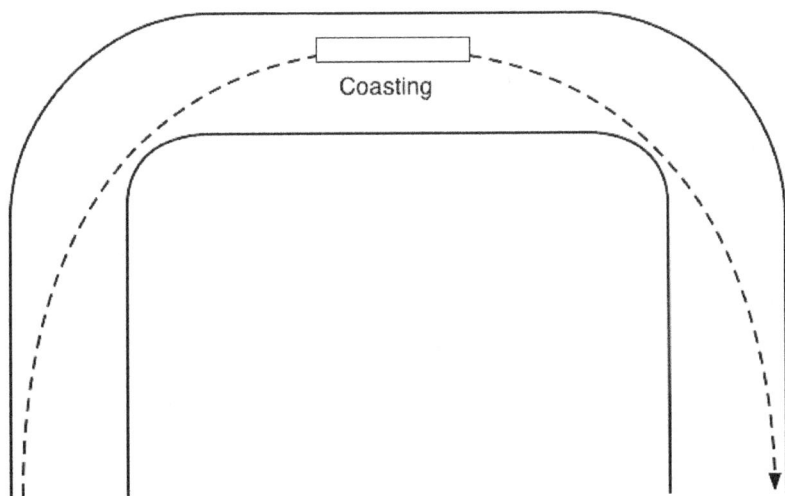

Figure N.6: Long Nadir

O is for Oversteer

Whenever you're aggressive, you're at the edge of mistakes.

-- Mario Andretti

Oversteer is the most common source of spins, off-track excursions, and collisions on the race track. There are many kinds of oversteer, but they all have one thing in common: the front tires have more traction than the rear tires. Most front-engined cars have more weight on the front than the rear while at rest, and are therefore prone to oversteer. On the street, you won't notice this imbalance because your car isn't sliding. But as soon as it starts to slide, the rear wheels will slide more than the fronts, causing the oversteer condition.

A little oversteer is not a bad thing. Advanced drivers prefer a car that oversteers to one that understeers. But to the novice driver unprepared for oversteer, it can be scary and dangerous. Controlling oversteer is one of the most important skills a driver can learn. It's sort of like hitting topspin in tennis. You can't really progress very far in the sport if you can't prevent the ball from flying out of bounds. Initial experiments with topspin may see balls sailing into the next court. And initial experiments with oversteer may involve some spinning.

The rest of this chapter describes typical sources of oversteer. Reading these descriptions will help you recognize and possibly avoid oversteer, but they won't help you deal with it when it happens. For that you need the muscle memory that comes from hours and hours of training.

Mid-corner Braking

If you're going around a corner and apply your brakes, the weight of the vehicle shifts forward. This adds grip to the front tires and takes away grip from the rear tires. If you're already sliding, you will oversteer. If you're not yet sliding, your rear tires may suddenly start to slide and whip around on you. Assuming you needed to brake, what can you do in this situation? Straighten the car out as much as possible while braking. Opening the steering wheel will decrease the side-loading on the car and allow you to swap longitudinal Gs for lateral Gs.

Trailing Throttle Oversteer

If you're sliding through a corner, the simple act of removing your foot from the throttle can cause you to spin. Just like mid-corner braking, trailing-throttle oversteer transfers weight and grip forward, just not as aggressively. But if you're driving at the limit, like you should be, every little change in balance changes the behavior of the car. Trailing throttle oversteer is not necessarily a bad thing and can help you rotate the car towards the apex. If you release the throttle and the back end starts to slide too much, you can recover either by adding throttle or by opening the wheel.

Power-on Oversteer

In a powerful RWD car, adding a lot of throttle can cause you to spin. Yes, you can get oversteer either with too much or too little throttle. In the case of too much throttle, it's not the weight of the car that is changing, but rather the coefficient of friction of the tires. If you spin your tires, their coefficient of friction drops precipitously and the result is more traction in the front than the rear.

Clutch-pop Oversteer

Generally, you want to make sure all your shifting is done before you enter a corner. If for some reason this doesn't happen and you decide to engage your clutch in the middle of a corner, watch out. The engine braking will shift your mass and traction forward. In a RWD car, you are also creating additional braking bias to the rear. If you engage the clutch too quickly or pop it, you could even spin while go down a straight.

Berms

The berms (aprons, gators, etc.) on the side of a track are often painted and have less grip than the rest of the track. This is especially true in the rain. This makes your car more prone to all kinds of oversteer, but especially power-on oversteer. Running over berms can also induce oversteer.

Bumps

A bumpy track can cause the entire car to temporarily lose loading. In a RWD car, the rear tires may suddenly spin and lose traction when doing so. Be careful through bumpy corners and don't mash the throttle to the floor. Even underpowered cars can lose traction when they are lightened by bumps.

Hand Brake Turn

Pulling the hand brake actuates only the rear brakes. It is therefore an excellent way to alter the brake bias towards the rear and induce oversteer. Locking the wheels will further add to the imbalance. Generally speaking, you should keep both hands on the wheel and not attempt to change your brake bias with the hand brake.

Scandinavian Flick

If you want to create oversteer, the best method is to combine some of the sources above with a driving technique called the *Scandinavian Flick* or *pendulum turn* (**Figure O.1**). This involves first turning in the opposite direction to load the suspension, and then quickly turning back in the intended direction of travel while using the throttle, brake, clutch or hand brake to create the front/rear imbalance. Throwing the car from one side to the other increases lateral acceleration and allows one to break the rear tires loose even at low speeds.

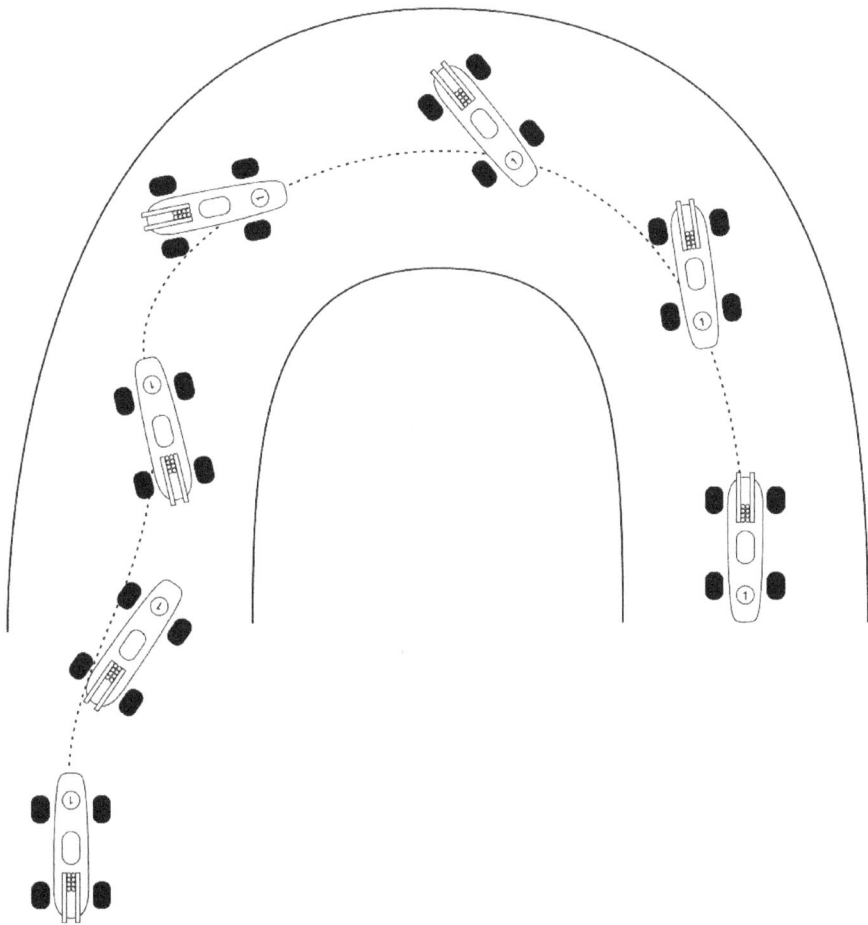

Figure O.1: The Scandinavian Flick

P is for Passing

Each time I'm leading a race and the driver behind challenges me, I can never be sure whether he's making a serious bid or not and that always puts me under pressure. When you're behind, on the other hand, it's best to time any move to perfection, and not to give the car ahead advance warning about what you're planning, so as to keep it a surprise.

-- Alain Prost

An amateur road race features a mixture of drivers. Some know the Formula 1 and NASCAR passing rules forwards and backwards, while others aren't even aware that there are rules. This is a book about amateur racing, not professional racing. So we're not going to discuss nuances. Instead, let's focus on you surviving the experiences of passing and getting passed.

Right of Way

The first car to the corner owns the corner.

In **Figure P.1**, car #1 is ahead of car #2 and has already turned into the corner. #1 owns the corner, and #2 has to give way.

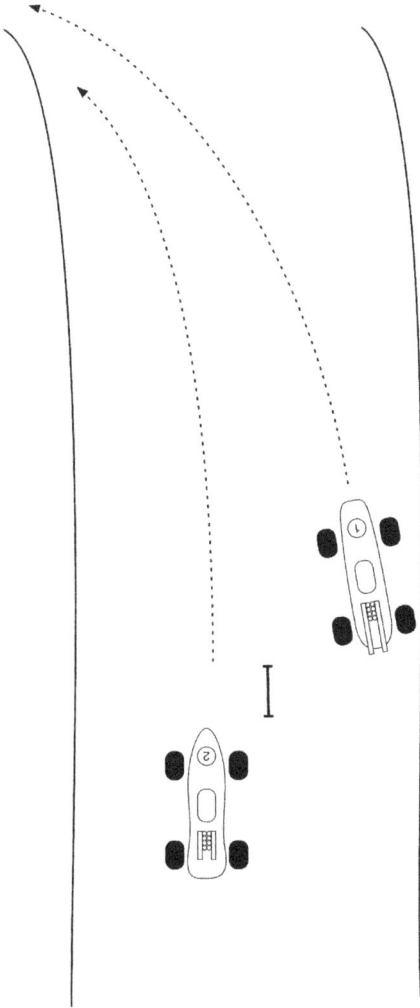

Figure P.1: First to turn

In **Figure P.2**, car #2 has **presented** itself along side car #1 in the **braking zone**. #2 owns the corner and #1 must give way.

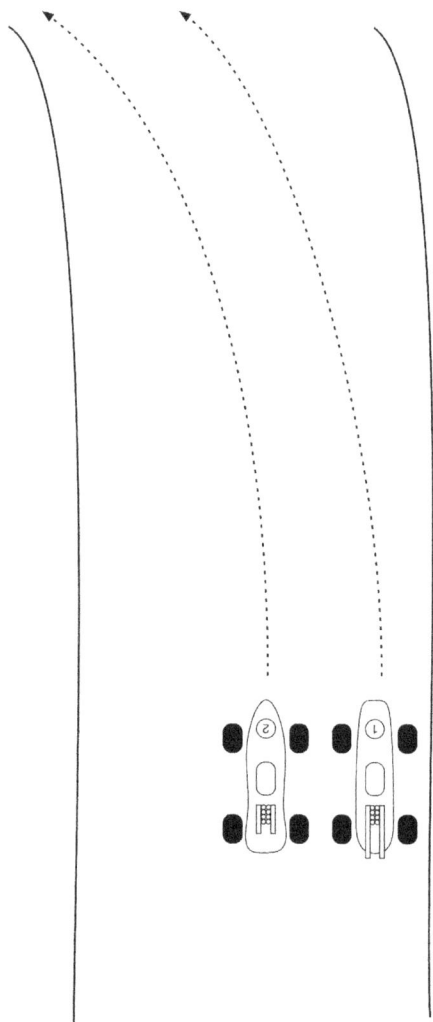

Figure P.2: Pulling even

In **Figure P.3**, both cars are turned in past the braking zone. Don't put yourself in this situation. Sort yourselves out in the braking zone, not in the corner.

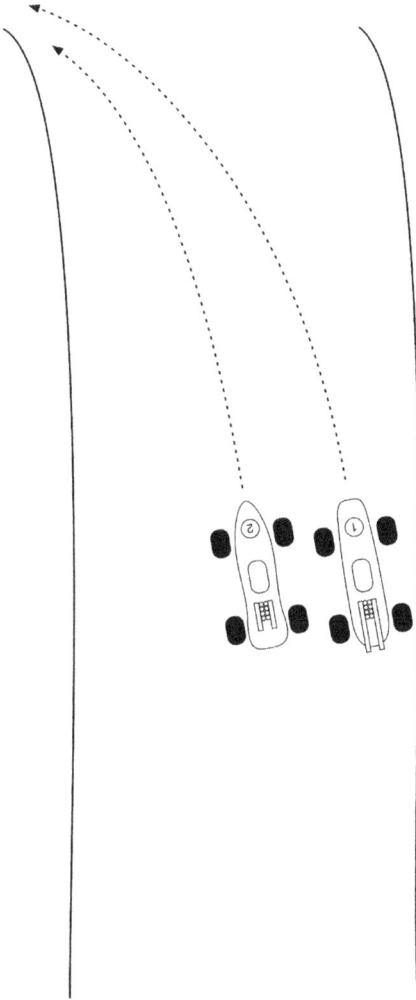

Figure P.3: Conflict

So let's say you establish right-of-way either by presenting yourself along side another car or by turning into the corner first. It's your corner. Let's further assume they hit you anyway and send you off track. You know what's more important than whose line it is? Whose car is still on track. If there's a reckless, oblivious, or incompetent driver near you, it's not the time to argue the finer points of right of way. Give them room and save your car from harm. Wait for your opportunity to pass as visibly and safely as possible.

Responsibility

It's the responsibility of the overtaking driver to make the pass cleanly.

If you're attempting to overtake someone, and you hit them in the process, it's your fault. That should be pretty obvious. But what if they hit you? If you put them in a bad situation, you didn't embrace your responsibility very well. Your pass is supposed to be a clean pass. **Don't use right of way as a shield. It won't protect you from harm.**

Getting Passed

There's nothing better than being in a close battle with an equally matched opponent. But if the car behind you is a lot faster, it's best to let it by as quickly and safely as possible. And then get on their tail and see if you can keep up. You might learn a thing or two and set your fastest lap of the day. Point them by if you can, but they aren't obliged to pass you where you want them to. Drive normally, but leave 1/2 car width on either side of you in case they sneak by while you're not looking.

Blocking

Blocking is the act of moving your car multiple times to prevent someone from passing. You are allowed to make one move to defend your position. Just one. Any more than that and you are blocking. Blocking is considered dishonorable. In an amateur race, most of the time what looks like blocking is usually some form of incompetence, like failing to check mirrors.

Q is for Quotes

I always have a quotation for everything - it saves original thinking.

-- Dorothy L. Sayers

The truth will set you free, but first it will piss you off.

-- Gloria Steinem

Racing

To finish first, you must first finish.

— Juan Manuel Fangio

I am not designed to come second or third. I am designed to win.

-- Ayrton Senna

The winner ain't the one with the fastest car, it's the one who refuses to lose.

— Dale Earnhardt

There are seven winners of the Monaco Grand Prix on the starting line today, and four of them are Michael Schumacher.

— Murray Walker

Driving the Limit

I don't know driving in another way which isn't risky. Each one has to improve himself. Each driver has its limit. My limit is a little bit further than others.

-- Ayrton Senna

SPEED SECRET: Race driver's job description: Drive the car to its limits, no more, no less.

-- Ross Bentley

My goal is not to be a race-car driver. The reason I'm racing is because I enjoy being in the car and being on the edge.
-- Jacques Villeneuve

During the race, try to drive a little faster than is enjoyable; you cannot go really fast without frightening yourself occasionally.
-- Paul Frère

If everything seems under control, you're just not going fast enough.
-- Mario Andretti

Your goal is to maximize your capabilities and those of the car... and not to exceed them!
-- Paul Dickinson

To achieve anything in this game you must be prepare to dabble in the boundary of disaster.
— Sterling Moss

Generally, those who function on bravery alone, and who take the most risks, are not the best drivers.
-- Alain Prost

It is a fact that nearly every car on any track can be driven quicker by someone else. It's all in your head... It's an intellectual exercise, not a bravery test.
 -- Peter Krause

Technique

When I look fast, I'm not smooth and I am going slowly. And when I look slow, I am smooth and going fast.

-- Alain Prost

Don't change gear unnecessarily. Every gear shift costs nearly a car's length, so it may be better to stay in a higher gear than to change down to get momentarily better acceleration, and then change up again. In case of doubt, always stay in the higher gear, you will be faster and strain the car less.

-- Paul Frère

You have really good car control, Too bad you have to use it all the time

-- Terry Earwood

To see everything, focus on nothing.

-- Peter Krause

Point-and-shoot versus momentum: All things being equal, they're equal.

-- Ross Bentley

Learning

It seems to me that analysis is hugely important. We have already seen that it is imperative to make as few mistakes as possible, but a driver will inevitably make some. It is essential then to analyse them and find out why they happened. Everything should be treated as a lesson, so that you are always making progress.

-- Alain Prost

If you are looking for perfect safety you will do well to sit on a fence and watch the birds, but if you really wish to learn you must mount a machine and become acquainted with its tricks by actual trial.

-- Wilbur Wright

Don't get in the way of the faster competitors, but when they have overtaken you, try to keep up with them as long as you can and watch their methods closely: you can learn a lot this way.

-- Paul Frère

Culture

No one — not rock stars, not professional athletes, not software billionaires, and not even geniuses — ever makes it alone.

-- Malcolm Gladwell

What is required is a level of discipline usually found only in Saints - which is admirable - together with a level of self confidence usually found only in very good con men - which is only partially admirable - and an inner selfishness that, in many ways, is not very admirable at all... I am not saying that racing drivers do no make good and loyal friends - they do... It is just that the racing driver's friends and mates must realize going in, that the driver will sell them down the river for a chance at a better ride. They may regret doing it, fleetingly, but do it they will - and they will not expect the act to materially affect the friendship. This is a way of life in which hard cuts soft.

-- Carroll Smith

The basic problem with motor racing as a profession is that it costs too much money to get good enough at it to get paid for doing it.

-- Carroll Smith

Racing is life. Everything that comes before or after is just waiting.

-- Steve McQueen

You can't make a race horse out of a pig, but you can make a very fast pig.

-- Bob Akin

If lightning strikes while you're in the car it's your fault.

-- Doc Bundy

Racing makes heroin addiction look like a vague longing for something salty

-- Peter Egan

Uncredited

Racing costs today exactly the same as it did twenty years ago... it takes every penny you have.

How do you make a small fortune in racing? Start with a large one.

You were absolutely hauling ass the last time I lapped you!

It is always easier to gain back a bit of speed in the middle of the corner than it is to get rid of a bit too much.

If you didn't crash, how do you know you were going as fast as you could?

I was doing fine until about mid-corner when I ran out of talent.

The most important thing to tune is the nut behind the wheel

R is for Rubber

If the car feels like it is on rails, you are probably driving too slow.

-- Ross Bentley

Your tires are one of the most important parts of your car. They are the source of grip and grip determines how fast you can go around a corner. Tires are made out of rubber, which turns out to be a very strange material. Understanding the properties of rubber will help you get the most out of your tires and car.

Friction

In physics class, you are taught that static friction is always greater than dynamic friction. You can observe this with a 2x4 and a washer. Raise the angle of the 2x4 and eventually the washer starts sliding. Now reduce the angle so it just stops. You've reached the limit of static friction. Now give the washer a little nudge. Once sliding, it keeps sliding. The coefficient of kinetic/dynamic friction is lower than static friction. Oddly, this isn't true of rubber. **Rubber has more when grip sliding than stationary**. That means your tires must be slipping a little for optimal grip.

The interaction of rubber with the road surface is critical. The most grip occurs when the surface is clean, dry, and has microscopically sharp edges. A clean and dry track adheres to the rubber best. The sharper the surface, the more *mechanical keying* there is. The movement of rubber across surface imperfections causes the rubber to change shape. This shape change provides grip even in the absence of adhesion (e.g. a wet track) and also causes the tire to heat up from the exercise its getting.

Slip Angle

A tire in a turn always has some slip. On the street, it may be so small that it's imperceptible, but it happens. The **slip angle** is the difference between the direction the wheel is pointed and the direction the wheel is traveling (**Figure R.1**). The tire is always turned into the corner more than the vehicle. Although the front tires are the only ones that turn, the rear tires are also experiencing a slip angle.

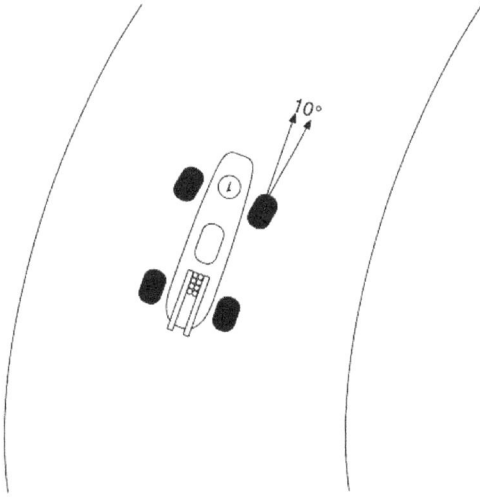

Figure R.1: Slip Angle

The optimal slip angle depends on the tire. Generally speaking, the more sporty the tire, the more slip angle it likes. The shape of the slip angle curve (**Figure R.2.**) is important. Although the grip falls off on either side of the slip angle, it falls off much more quickly on the low side. So if you are going to err on one side or the other, it's better to have too much slip. However, most novice racers drive a low slip angle because they are unaccustomed to driving a sliding car (see "M is for Muscle Memory").

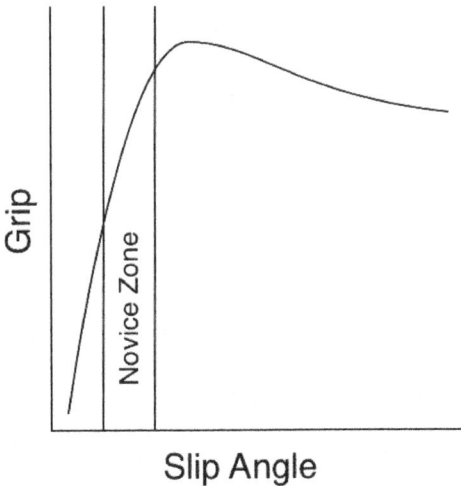

Figure R.2: Grip vs. Slip Angle

Heat

Grip depends on temperature (**Figure R.3**). If your tires are too cold or too hot, you won't be able to go as fast. The optimal temperature and the shape of the curve depend on the tire. The optimal temperature is hotter than you might guess and most novice racers don't get their tires to the optimal temperature because they aren't driving with enough slip angle.

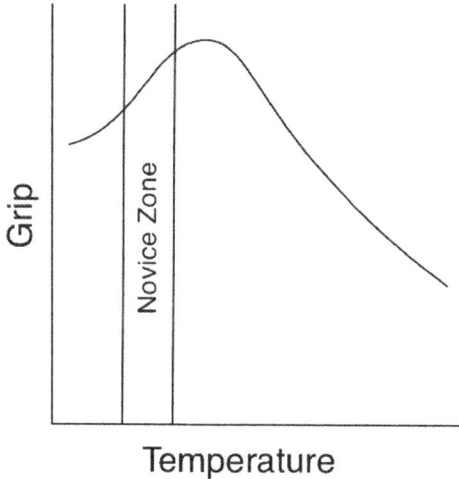

Figure R.3: Grip vs. Temperature

Braking is an effective way to heat your tires. But braking too hard to the point where the tires smoke is bad. That means you locked the wheels and overheated the tires. Not only is the grip lower, the tires will become flat spotted.

Load

In the theoretical world, doubling the weight on a tire doubles its grip. Unfortunately, rubber doesn't work that way. The more you increase the load on the tire, the less it returns to you in friction (**Figure R.4**). A lighter car corners faster than a heavier car because its tires experience less load. If you distribute the weight over a larger tire area, you can mitigate this effect somewhat. This is why wider tires are often faster than narrower ones. But it also takes more effort to heat up a wider tire, and wider tires tend to weigh more. So the optimal tire size is a bit of a compromise.

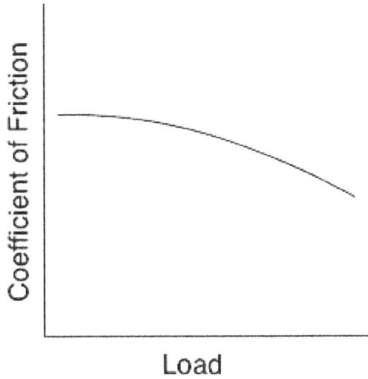

Figure R.4: Friction vs. Load

Another way to improve grip is to distribute load more evenly. The higher the roll center, and the looser the suspension, the more weight is transferred from side to side on cornering and front to back on braking. So a stiffer and lower suspension improves traction by keeping the weight more equally on all the tires.

S is for Simulation

Let's take flight simulation as an example. If you're trying to train a pilot, you can simulate almost the whole course. You don't have to get in an airplane until late in the process.

--Roy Romer

Racing has been a popular genre of video game from the beginning, but in recent years the hardware and software have improved to the point where it's no longer a game, but a simulation, and a bona fide training tool.

A simulator rig includes:

- Software (which we don't belittle by calling it a video game)
- Computer
- Controllers (steering wheel, pedals, shifter)
- Cockpit

Software

The best simulator software is currently iRacing (**Figure S.1**). The subscription cost is about $6 per month. The service comes with 12 cars and 14 tracks, and you can buy additional ones for $10-15 each. The default cars are fine, but you'll probably want others just for fun. Get a lot of tracks because each one poses different challenges. Again, if you're looking at these prices and thinking it's expensive, then either your priorities are messed up or you should find a different sport. If you're going to be racing on a real race track, for safety's sake (yours and everyone around you), do your due diligence and make your simulator investment a priority.

Figure S.1: iRacing

Why iRacing? Because your actions on track matter. Your *Safety Rating* determines which racing series you can drive in. If you're completely unsafe, you will never get out of the rookie ranks. The only way to drive the advanced cars is by proving that you're a safe driver. Your *iRating* is an estimate of your skill level. Every time you race, your iRating is at stake. The combination of Safety Rating and iRating identify what kind of racer you are. And there's no hiding behind an avatar. When you sign up, you have to use your real name. Every time you hit the track, it's your skill and reputation on display. Racing cars is serious business. To get the most out of simulation training, be just a serious in a virtual car and a real car.

Aside from iRacing there are a couple other good simulators. Assetto Corsa and rFactor 2 are similarly realistic, but their communities are not as large and there are fewer cars and tracks. The original rFactor is still useable and much cheaper, but the graphics will appear very dated in comparison. Console games like Forza and Gran Tourismo cater more to the gamer than the simulator. They are still useful though, especially when using a steering wheel rather than a hand controller.

Computer

When you peer into your monitor, the distances you see on the screen should look like real life distances. For this reason you need a large, widescreen monitor for a realistic field of view (FOV). If you have a small monitor or a TV placed across the room from you, your ability to accurately judge the distance to the next corner will be impaired. You want your FOV to be as realistic as possible, and this means putting a large widescreen monitor right behind your steering wheel and then setting the FOV in the simulator to the correct angle based on the width of the monitor and the distance from your eyes to the screen. The really serious *simmers* wrap 3 monitors around their cockpit, but this requires a larger computer investment. Soon, people will trade triple monitors for 3D virtual reality goggles like the Oculus Rift. If you're thinking this sounds too involved for a video game, you're right: this is not a game, it's simulation.

Controllers

The single most important part of your controller rig is the steering wheel. It must be able to transmit realistic forces to your hands. This is your muscle memory training, and it will not only get you out of typical oversteer spins, it will also make you faster through every corner. Logitech, Thrustmaster, and Fanatec are the most popular brands. Spend a little more to buy a 3 pedal kit because it helps you learn heel-toe shifting. An H-pattern shifter is also nice to have, but it is the least important part of your rig.

The brake pedal is the most important pedal in the car, but has a very unrealistic feel on most controllers. The brake pedal in your car is pressure-sensitive but most controllers use a potentiometer and spring, making the pedal mostly distance-sensitive. You can buy kits to convert Logitech and Thrustmaster pedals into pressure-sensitive devices. Some of these even use hydraulics, just like your car. Fanatec pedals have load cells already built into them. If you're serious about using a simulator for training, you should get a pressure-sensitive brake pedal.

Your controllers can easily be your greatest expense, but they don't need to be. You can find used controllers on Craigslist, Ebay, or the iRacing forum for much less than new. But be warned that some parts can wear out and you may need to do some minor repairs.

Cockpit

Do you need a cockpit? No. But every time you sit down for a training session, you should be taking it seriously, and a cockpit with a similar layout to your race car will put you in the proper frame of mind. You can purchase a purpose-built sim cockpit or build your own using someone else's plans or your own imagination. The iRacing forum has hundreds of examples of people who have built impressive cockpits from wood, metal, or PVC.

My Rig

My simulator rig is cobbled together from various parts purchased used or heavily discounted. My computer is an older desktop I had that I upgraded with a more recent graphics card and a 1080p monitor. My wheel is a Logitech Driving Force GT. The shifter and pedals come from a Logitech G25, but they are connected with their own dedicated USB connections (improves the resolution of the pedals). I have also replaced the brake pedal with a PerfectPedal hydraulic unit, which was approximately half the price of my entire rig. My cockpit is constructed from spare lumber, and old table, and the castoff seat from a BMW E30. Total outlay was the price of a couple track days.

Training

How should you use your simulator to train? Like any sport, it's not just the hours you put in, but how you put those hours in. If you watch professional athletes train, they don't goof around and they don't limit their activity to matches. They do drills to work on improving specific skills. That would make a great sequel to this book... watch for it.

Amateurs practice until they get it right, professionals practice until they can't get it wrong.

--Various

T is for Track Maps

We're all pilgrims on the same journey - but some pilgrims have better road maps.

-- Nelson DeMille

There are few activities more fun or useful than scribbling on a track map with a bunch of friends. You can download a line drawing for most tracks at their websites. Print these out and bring them with you to the track. Have a track map, clipboard, and pen ready to scribble notes as soon as you leave the track. A line drawing itself doesn't itself show much detail, but you can make it come alive now and later by drawing on it.

- Indicate where you brake for each turn.
- Show areas that are on or off camber
- Indicate areas that are good passing zones
- Indicate areas that are risky passing zones
- Identify potentially dangerous areas
- Mark where you change gears

These exercises will help you cement reference points in your mind. They are also excellent talking points with other drivers.

Being a nerdy person, I like to annotate track maps on a computer. **Figure T.1** shows a track mack I made for my team when Thunderhill added an additional 2 miles. Green lines indicate full throttle. White lines are partial throttle. Red lines are braking zones. In addition to turn numbers, I indicated specific areas of interest with letters. Here's how I annotated Thunderhill West for a Miata.

Figure L.1: Track map example

T1W

T1W is a high speed kink followed by a slow off camber carousel. It is one of the most fun corners on the entire track. As you pass start/finish and head towards T1W, you should set up track right to get ready for the left-hand kink. Be prepared for fast cars and slow drivers to brake on the way in, but the braking zone is actually well past the kink. You may find it settling (mentally and physically) to lift at the entry. Do not brake and do not downshift. The kerb at **A** is generous and flat, and you can really straighten this out by driving over it. Once your wheels hit the curbing on the right side, brake very hard in a straight line and downshift to 3rd if you were previously in 4th. Trail-brake around the initial part of the carousel and then balance throttle and steering as the car turns uphill. If you're not careful, you can overspeed this corner and the off-camber will send you off the track. Watch for cars entering the track at **B**.

T2W

T2W is a half ascending, half descending 180° carousel that is mostly on camber. Unlike the T3 carousel on the East side, you can't simply make the car take a set and then progressively add throttle. The turn descends half way around, and the added gravity as well as pitch of the hill will make your car oversteer. For this reason, you can take this corner as a double apex. This is a great corner to practice your countersteering. As the turn opens up and you see the following straight, go to full throttle. But watch out at the exit because the track has no apron at **C** and you can go off track here if you're not careful.

T3W

The preceding straight is downhill and the fastest part of the track. As you set up for T3W on the right side of the track, make sure you don't drop 2 wheels in the dirt. There are three common ways through this corner. The scared driver brakes way too early, downshifts to 3rd, and wiggles through. The foolish driver brakes way too late, downshifts to 3rd, and wiggles through. The fast driver stays in 4th, barely brushes the brakes, and flies straight through. Focus on the apex after the kink, marked **D**, and keep your speed as high as possible. Shifting to 3rd will overslow the car, and you may find yourself upshifting to 4th and then back to 3rd after the kink. Just leave it in the high gear. The apron is very bumpy at the kink, so I try to avoid it.

T4W

T4W is an off camber, blind, uphill corner with a mid-track entry and a dangerous exit. It's the most critical corner on the track in a momentum car. After flying through the kink at T3W, you have to get the car completely balanced and at the optimal speed and angle. Make the braking zone long and gentle so that you can balance the side loading of the car as you transition from brakes to throttle. They key to this corner is getting to full throttle as soon as possible. If you overslow the car, the uphill will sap your speed and ruin the high speed esses. If you overspeed the car, you will run wide at the exit and drop wheels at **E**. The apron here is more generous than it used to be, but you can still drop wheels to ill effect. The dirt is soft, and it can get dug out over the course of a race. Driving across such a bump at high speed could brake suspension components.

T5W

The esses of T5W are 100% full throttle. You can straighten them out a little if by taking a wide entry on the first right-hander, but it's not really necessary. Run over the smooth aprons. You will probably run out of gearing near the end, so short-shifting to 4th somewhere in the middle is appropriate. The esses are a good place to pass offpace cars if you make sure the other drivers see you.

T6W

T6W is a high speed 90° left-hander that is slightly off camber with blind exit. The key to the corner is not throwing away all that speed you had in the esses. The difficulty is that you might run out of track at the blind exit. It's just as fast to take this in 4th gear and kinder to the car, so don't downshift to 3rd. Brake gently and very gradually trail off the brakes to set your corner speed. There may be some coasting involved. Add throttle gently as your round the corner. You can't see the track swing left at **F** and it's very easy to go 4 off if you add too much throttle too soon. It's a safe place to go dirt tracking, but you may earn a black flag doing so.

T7W

T7W is a very sharp hairpin corner. Most people brake way too early. Start your braking just after you hit the left side of the track at **G**. The key is to get the car rotated quickly under trail-braking so that the car is straight and 100% throttle as soon as possible. There's not much momentum you can conserve here, so it's all about getting the power down.

T8W

Although it's not a critical corner, it is one of the more entertaining ones. The apex is blind and the car will get quite light as it crests the hill. Setting up far track left will straighten the corner out and improve the traction over the top, but it's just as fast to stay farther right and slide a bit. The straight before the next corner is so slow that it doesn't really matter how you exit T8W.

T9W & T10W

Coming down from 8 you will have some good speed, so T9W is a heavy braking zone. It's another very sharp hairpin that benefits from trail-braking and early throttle application. The exit line depends on how they set up T10W. If there are cones at **H** that force you to the left side of the track, you have to sacrifice the exit of T9W to get a good late apex line at T10W. But if the cones aren't there, you can get a better run through T9W and then a higher speed early apex at T10W. Just don't run into the pit wall.

U is for Understeer

Oversteer scares passengers. Understeer scares drivers.

-- Uncredited

Understeer occurs when your front tires have less grip than your rear tires. If you turn your steering wheel and nothing seems to happen, it's probably a case of understeer.

The rest of this chapter describes typical sources of understeer. Reading these descriptions will help you recognize and possibly avoid understeer, but they won't help you deal with it when it happens. For that you need the muscle memory that comes from hours and hours of training (see "M is for Muscle Memory").

Over-Braking Understeer

The most common way to experience understeer is to brake too hard and then try to turn your steering wheel. If all of your traction is being used for braking, there's none left for turning. This is especially true if your front tires are locked in a skid. In **Figure U.1.**, the driver has misjudged the entry speed, jams on his brakes, and continues in the same direction even though the wheels are turned. Letting off the brakes will restore some steering, but if the driver has come in way too hot, he is still headed off track.

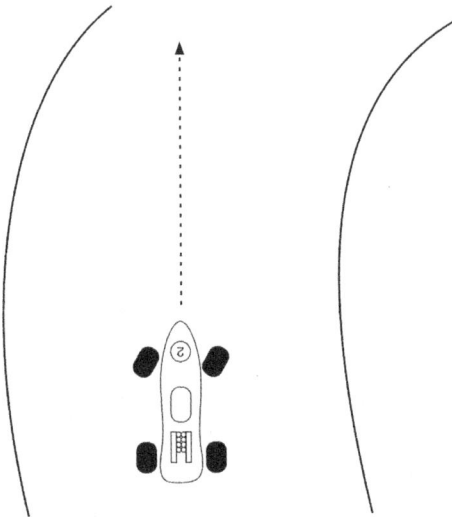

Figure U.1: Understeer corner entry

In **Figure U.2.** car #1 has spun in front of car #2. In response, car #2 jams on the brakes but still keeps going straight because there's no traction left for steering. Both driver #1 and driver #2 are doing #1 or #2 in their pants about now. By releasing some braking, driver #1 can restore steering and avoid the accident, but will probably end up off track. That's preferable to wrecking two cars.

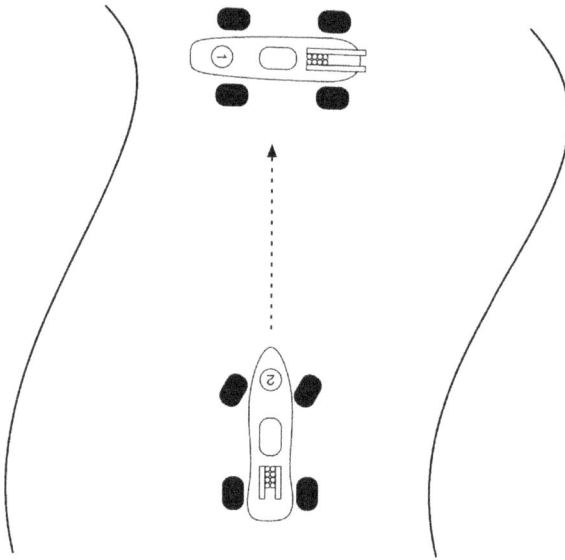

Figure U.2: Impending doom

Although you can stop in a shorter distance without ABS, the positives of ABS outweigh the negatives: you can keep steering and you won't flat-spot your tires. If your car has ABS, don't delete it.

Power-on Understeer

When you accelerate, weight and grip shift to the rear of the car. This can cause the front tires to lose traction which results in understeer. This situation is exacerbated by cars with engines behind the driver because the front end is light by design. The most common situation to experience this kind of understeer is accelerating too aggressively on corner exits.

Even though front-wheel drive cars have a lot of weight on their front tires, they can be prone to understeer if they have powerful motors.

Spinning tires have very little traction, so jamming on the throttle can see you sliding off track very easily.

Fortunately, there is a very simple response to power-on oversteer: slow down. Simply reducing the throttle will shift weight forward and restore balance, or in the case of a spinning tire, restore traction.

Steering Lock Understeer

Optimal traction requires a specific slip angle (see "R is for Rubber"). If you exceed that angle, traction fades. When novice drivers find themselves understeering in a corner, their automatic response is to turn the steering wheel even more. This doesn't work! In fact, because the slip angle is too great, they make the situation worse. To restore steering, one must slow down or open the wheel.

Elevation

Going uphill shifts the balance of the car to the rear. This makes you more prone to all kinds of understeer. It can be a little frightening if you mix turning with accelerating or braking on an uphill section of track. If you find yourself losing traction, straighten out the car as much as possible and use maintenance throttle.

V is for Vehicle

If I had all the money I spent on cars... I'd spend it all on cars.

-- Scott Fisher

Rent, Build, or Buy?

Renting a car for the day is surprisingly expensive... until you add up all the costs of buying or building your own racecar. Then it starts to look pretty reasonable. Owning a racecar only makes sense if you actually enjoy working on cars. It doesn't save much money.

Building a racecar takes money and time. You will spend thousands of dollars and hundreds of hours on the build, and the end result is something you can't easily sell. As a general rule, you can sell a racecar for less than 1/4 of what it costs to build (in parts, labor is free). For this reason, if you're just starting out, you can get a real bargain buying someone else's racecar. It doesn't have to be a competitive car to be fun. If you really love racing, your first car will probably not be your last. So don't try to make the first car the perfect car.

Choosing Your Car

Cheap, fast and reliable. Pick two.

You will get a lot of admiring looks if you bring something obscure or expensive to the track. There's a saying that there are people who drive their cars and people who wash their cars. This is a book for drivers, so if you want to show off in something fancy, I don't have a lot of advice. I can tell you that depending on what car you choose, you could spend 90% of your time driving or 90% wrenching (our team started with a car that required 90% wrenching and it was very frustrating for this driver). Some cars are notoriously fragile and even professional mechanics have a hard time keeping them going. If you want to do a lot of driving, make your track car something very reliable and common.

One of the best cars to start with is an older Mazda Miata. They are mechanically robust and forgiving at the limit. They have no bad manners to speak of. Plus, there are so many of them at any given track day, that if something goes wrong, spare parts and expert knowledge is generally easy to come by. Another excellent choice is a BMW 3-series. If your track car pulls double duty as a street car, a BMW might be a better choice because of the storage room. But after you have upgraded the suspension for track use, it's really not a very good street car anymore anyway.

Harnesses & Rollover Protection

While many track day driving organizations will allow you to drive with typical 3 point over-one-shoulder seat belts, these are not as safe as racing harnesses. If you decide to purchase harnesses, and you should if you're going to take track driving seriously, then you also need racing seats and a roll bar or roll cage.

In a standard car, you can move around a bit when belted in. This isn't very good for safety or car control, but if the roof collapses, you aren't trapped by the harness. As soon as you put harnesses on, you're stuck where you are, so you need a stronger structure to protect your head in the case of a roll-over.

If you plan on driving your car on the street, a full cage can be dangerous because your skull could hit the roll bar. Even when fully padded this can be a problem. So if you're driving to and from the track in a fully caged car, put your helmet on. A roll bar is behind you, and doesn't create the same safety problems on the street. So for a street & track car, a roll bar is the best choice. It won't be legal to race though.

There are 3 recommended configurations.

1. Street: standard belts and seats, helmet on track
2. Autocross: roll bar, harness, racing seat, helmet on track
3. Race: full cage, harness, racing seat, helmet always

Fire

Racecars occasionally catch on fire. A fire extinguisher is therefore mandatory safety equipment. A fire suppression system that sprays the engine and cockpit with fire retardant chemicals at the pull of a handle is also a good idea. Don't skimp on safety. You will drive more confidently and better knowing you and your car are safe.

Mirrors

One of the most common sources of accidents in amateur racing is drivers failing to use their mirrors. Your side mirrors should be adjusted to see cars beside you, not behind you (**Figure V.1**).

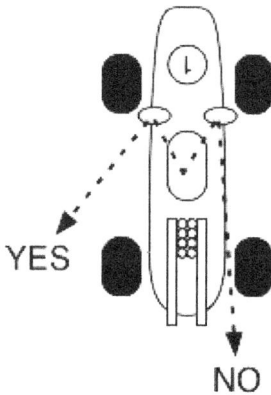

Figure V.1: Side Mirrors

If you're keeping track of everyone around you, you should be able to predict when faster cars behind you will attempt to pass. But don't be overconfident in your ability to monitor traffic and decide to remove your side mirrors to improve your aerodynamic efficiency. Safety first. And in that vein, adding a panoramic rearview mirror can help you monitor the cars around you.

Performance

Simplify, then add lightness

-- Colin Chapman

Removing all unnecessary weight from your car will make it handle better and use less consumables (fuel, tires, brake pads). It's also free. So start there. After that, make the car as comfortable to drive as possible. You'll get better at driving and be safer doing it. I think the whole point of performance driving is to improve the performance of the driver. If you're trying to figure out what to spend some extra cash on, ask yourself, "does this make me better or the car better?"

Tuning

I have heard expert and completely opposite opinions about slotted rotors, high octane, ride height, anti-roll bars, tire pressures, nitrogen vs. air, supercharger vs. turbo etc. There's so much information and mis-information in racing that it's hard to know what to believe. Ask 5 experts and you may get 6 opinions. Many parts of a vehicle are reasonably well understood in isolation, but changes in one part of a vehicle can affect others. For example, lowering a car reduces its drag and roll center, which are generally desirable qualities. But lowering also changes the suspension geometry and could cause the suspension to bottom-out over bumps. Tuning a car is difficult because **everything affects everything else**. You will often get the advice to change only one thing at a time while tuning. That's good advice if you want to see how a single change affects the car, but the optimal combination of parameters may require compromises. In other words, by optimizing one thing at a time, you may never find the optimal combination. There are plenty of books about tuning, but until you can drive a car at the limit and feel how it behaves there, you have more important things to be doing than tuning.

FWD vs RWD

There are a lot of drivers who think that all racecars should be rear wheel drive (RWD). I'm not one of them. Front wheel drive (FWD) cars are just as much fun to drive at the limit, they just require a slightly different driving technique. When you accelerate in a FWD car, the weight shifts rearward, away from the drive wheels. If you stomp on the throttle, the car will spin its front tires, reducing their grip, and lowering your exit speed. For this reason, trail-braking and smooth throttle control are absolutely essential. Trail-braking helps rotate the car earlier in the corner so that weight can be distributed to both front wheels as soon as possible. Smooth throttle control prevents the front tires from slipping too much, and losing traction. You want to trail-brake and accelerate smoothly in a RWD vehicle too, but a FWD is not as forgiving when you get it wrong.

Cheating

If your driving passion finds you in a racing series with rules, expect some competitors to break them. Some people would never cheat. Some do it as a way of giving 110% effort, or to show their engineering cleverness, or because they assume everyone else is already cheating. Personally, I'm not inclined to cheat. I'd probably do more harm than good in the attempt, and I like fighting against the odds.

At some point in every racer's life he has to make his peace with cheating. I do not approve of cheating ... at all. Of course, like every successful racer, I differentiate between taking advantage of loopholes in the regulations, stretching the grey areas and outright cheating. In any given racing series I will not start the cheating. If someone else starts it, I will appeal to them and to the officials to stop it. If my efforts do not succeed, then I'll show them how it is done ....

-- Carroll Smith, Drive to Win

W is for Why

The most exciting phrase to hear in science, the one that heralds new discoveries, is not 'Eureka!' but 'That's funny...'

--Isaac Asimov

To get better at driving, you must approach it with the curiosity of a child and the rigor of a scientist. You must ask the question 'why' over and over. But asking why isn't nearly enough. You also need the tools to examine your driving or you will never get the answers.

Some 1500 years ago when bubonic plague was killing millions of people, there was no way of knowing it was caused by the bacterium *Yersinia pestis*. The microscope would not be invented for more than 1000 years and the germ theory of disease would lag another 300 years. They had absolutely no way of observing bacteria, and even if they could, they had no way of understanding what they would see. Truly the dark ages.

Fortunately for you, we live in an age where the tools (hardware and software) to analyze driving are easy to obtain. There are 3 general categories: video cameras, predictive lap timers, and data loggers. Each one has its role in driver development.

Video Cameras

All racecars should have at least 1 video camera running all the time. If you only have 1 camera, this should be mounted in the middle of the vehicle with a view out the front that also captures the driver. If you position the camera cleverly, you can also see out the rearview and wing mirrors. Video cameras are not there just for your vanity. It is awesome sharing your best laps with you friends, of course, but their real utility is as a learning tool. Video cameras are also great to settle arguments about who was at fault in an incident, and for this reason some racing series require each car to have a video camera.

Predictive Lap Timers

A predictive timer compares your current pace to your previous performances. If you've been training in iRacing, you know this as the red/green bar on your display that shows if you're going slower (red) or faster (green) than your previous best sector.

The reason a predictive timer is useful is because it provides immediate feedback on your driving. You might accidentally take an earlier apex and find that it improves your lap time. Or you might make a clumsy shift and see that it loses 0.3 seconds immediately and another 1.2 on the following straight. Even more usefully, you can use it to answer live experiments. You can ask "what if I move my brake release 3 meters back?" or "what if I stay in 4th instead of dropping to 3rd?"

One of the best predictive timers is the RumbleStrip DLT1-GPS. It is simple, robust, and highly visible with bright red LEDs. It displays speed and lap delta in a few different configurations. Part of the appeal is that it's so simple. Even technophobes love it.

Figure W.1: RumbleStrip DLT1-GPS

Data Loggers

Data loggers are used to review and analyze your driving after you get out of the car. In the simplest case, they record GPS position, speed, and G-forces. In that regard, they aren't much different than a predictive timer, except that they store all of your laps for downloading into a computer. From there, you can compare laps to each other to find out where you're fast and slow. One of the best uses for data loggers is comparing the lap times of different drivers. Each driver has a unique style, and the differences between them can be very illuminating.

An essential part of a data logger package is the software used to view the laps. Since you'll be spending a lot of time looking at laps, you might choose the data logger based on which software you like best. One of the most popular data logger packages is the

TraqMate/TrackView from Track Systems Technologies (**Figure W. 2**).

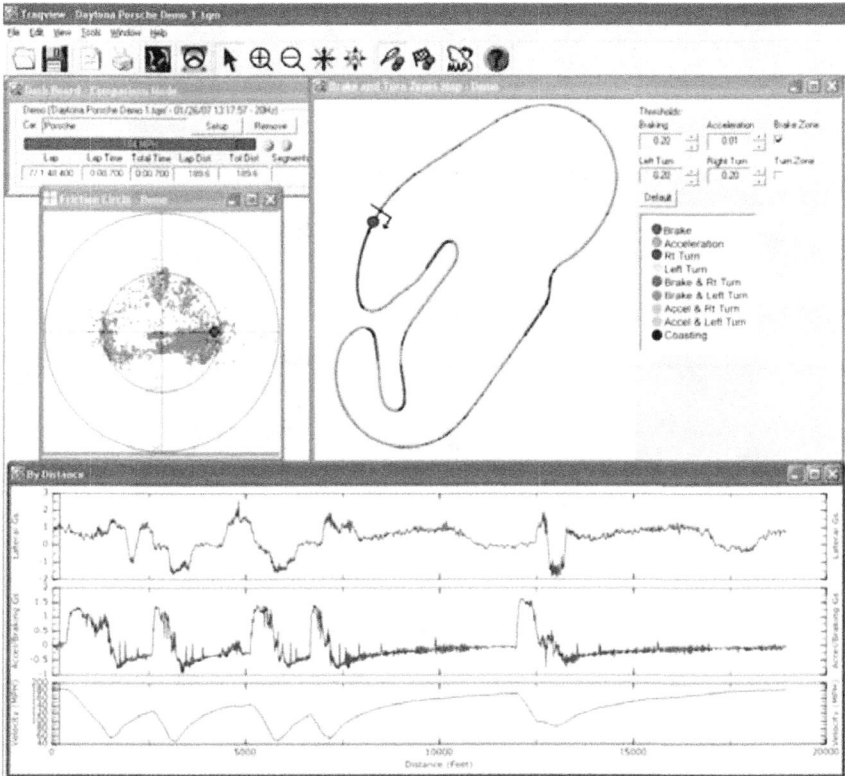

Figure W.2: TraqView Software

Data loggers generally have configurable inputs that let you record vital statistics from your car such as oil pressure/temperature, water temperature, voltage, brake pressure, steering angle, air:fuel ratio, etc. Some data acquisition systems have sophisticated displays that replace the standard gauges with a color LCD (**Figure W.3.**).

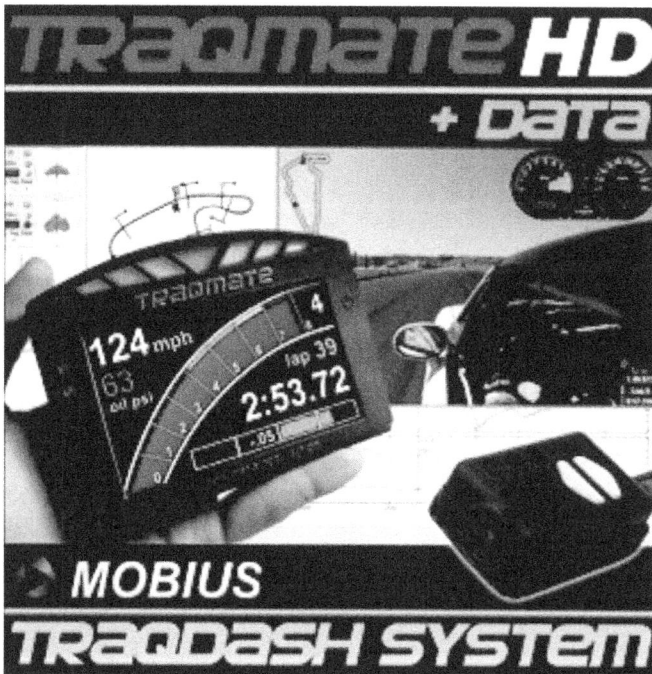

Figure W.3: TraqMate System

For more information, visit the web pages of AiM Sports, Autosport Labs, RacePak, Race Technology, RumbleStrip Racing Products and Track Systems Technology.

Smartphones

One of the least expensive and most convenient telemetry systems is simply a smartphone. They have a video camera, GPS antenna, and accelerometers built in. It's everything you need except the software to tie it all together. Fortunately, such software already exists in the form of Harry's Lap Timer, CMS Lap Timer, and TrackAddict (and more). If you get an OBDII reader that transmits to your phone, you can overlay throttle position, air fuel mixture, voltage, etc. It's an inexpensive and convenient solution. Unfortunately, the sensors in phones are not very accurate and OBDII has a low sampling rate not really designed for racing. It's either barely acceptable or barely unacceptable depending on your perspective.

Autosport Labs recently announced the *Race Capture* (**Figure W. 4.**), a new product that communicates high resolution GPS, accelerometers, and CAN bus data to a smartphone/tablet. This appears to be a more than acceptable telemetry solution for the budget-minded racer, but it requires a newer car for full functionality.

Figure W.4: Race Capture

X is for X-Factor

You need to be comfortable being uncomfortable

--Ross Bentley

What is the most important quality for a racer to develop? In "Ultimate Speed Secrets", and elsewhere, Ross Bentley talks a lot getting comfortable with being uncomfortable. What exactly is he talking about? What's so uncomfortable about racing? It's supposed to be a source of fun, not discomfort, right? I believe there are 4 major sources of discomfort: (1) speed (2) G-force (3) sliding (4) traffic. Getting comfortable with these discomforts is hard work and requires patience and perseverance. Part of what makes racing so much fun is that it isn't easy.

Without hard work, nothing grows but weeds.

-- Gordon B. Hickley

Speed

Going fast is thrilling, but it's also a little scary. Some drivers are afraid of their cars. Having a healthy respect for speed isn't a bad thing. Safety is more important than lap times. Don't go beyond what you feel is safe. Don't get bullied into going faster than you're comfortable with. And if you're in a street car that doesn't have a full roll cage, fire system, harnesses, and 38.1 neck brace, don't take large risks. You will get more and more comfortable with speed every time you're on track. It's a long learning process for some. Push yourself a little, but not a lot. There are more important things than lap times.

G-Force

Some people are afraid to drive with high G-forces. They might be perfectly fine going 140 mph down a straight, but then they park it in the corners. There's really nothing unsafe about high G-forces. Unlike speed, high G-forces aren't going to kill you. Go to a skid pad and drive around in circles faster and faster. Eventually you will relax into the seat and enjoy the sound of chirping tires. It may take a while, but work hard you must, if fear you will master.

Sliding

You can stare at graphs all day that show you rubber grips best when sliding a little bit, but that doesn't change the fact that when your front tires start to slide, the steering wheel goes light in your hands and you no longer feel connected to the track. Turning the wheel doesn't do much, so you slow down to a speed where it does. You have to get beyond this stage because racecars are supposed to slide, and your job as a driver is to find the optimal slip. It's easy for me to say, but I know it's not easy to do. If you can't drive a light wheel comfortably, it's because you don't have enough seat time. It's easiest, cheapest, and safest to gain that time via simulation (see "S is for Simulation"). The force-feedback in most wheels is accurate enough to train your muscle memory.

Traffic

Racing wheel to wheel with other drivers is about the most exciting thing there is. It's also unnerving. What are the drivers in front, behind, and to the side of you going to do? If you've never been on a race track before, you might not know what to expect. This is another situation where simulation time is very useful. People tend to drive more dangerously in simulation than they do on a real track. So it's a good place to build up your knowledge of stupid driving. You'll feel a lot more comfortable in real life when you've experienced the same situation hundreds of times in simulation.

Y is for Y Chromosome

Since I started in motor racing I've worked with people from all over the world. We are all here to go racing and prejudice will never play any part in that.

-- Kimi Raikkonen

If you're reading this book, odds are, you've got a Y chromosome. Why? Simply because there are a lot more men than women in motorsports. Why is racing so male-dominated? There are a lot of explanations, some of which have merit and others which do not. Racing is also dominated by whites and people with money. This is true at every level. Let's not get into speculative reasons for how this came to be or why it is maintained and instead focus on the consequences.

A room full of rich white men is not very welcoming to anyone who isn't a rich white man.

If you're white and want to experience what *unwelcome* feels like, join an all black pickup basketball game. Most of the players won't care what you look like. They care more that you can hit an open jump shot. But you'll feel awkward and a little out of place even if you are a decent player. Now imagine being a novice.

Feeling unwelcome is a problem. You won't perform your best, which could make you less safe on track, and you won't enjoy the experience as much. We don't want racing to be unwelcoming to anyone. Racing is too much fun to make it exclusive. Racing deserves broader participation and you can help make that happen.

Man Up

What can you do to make the racing environment more welcoming? You have to go out of your way to be helpful. It's not enough for you to mind your own business. If you're not actively breaking the *club* atmosphere, you're silently contributing to it. Unfortunately, being shy can sometimes be construed as being aloof.

If you see someone who looks a little uncomfortable, break the ice and introduce yourself. Find out if they've been to the track before. Compliment them on their car (whatever it is). Talk about which turns are your favorites. Tell them about that time you went off track because you did something stupid. Making a little fun of yourself is always friendlier than boasting about your lap times.

Man Down

What can you do to make yourself less unintentionally unwelcoming? Turn down the volume. Don't talk so loud. Don't joke so much. Don't draw attention to yourself. Don't talk about what a great driver you are and how your buddy always messes up the exit of 7. Banter among equals can strengthen relationships, but among those at different levels, banter serves to widen social gaps.

You're at the track to have fun and forget the problems in daily life. So is everyone else. Don't ruin other peoples' fun with the spillover of yours. There are certain topics you should stay away from. Don't discuss or make jokes about politics, religion, income, or sex. There's absolutely no place for phrases like "so-and-so drives like a _____".

Z is for Zzzzz

Fatigue makes cowards of us all.

--Vince Lombardi

The consequences of stepping out of bounds on a basketball court are very different from a race track. Racing is insanely dangerous even under the best circumstances. One of the best ways to protect yourself is by being well rested.

Fatigue

Driving tired is much like driving drunk. Your reflexes are slow and your judgement is poor. Although their methods are not always up the standards of professional scientists, the MythBusters conducted a informative and entertaining episode (#152: Tipsy vs. Tired) comparing drunk and tired driving. Under their conditions (excessive sleep deprivation vs. a few drinks), they found that driving tired was far worse than driving drunk.

A more scientific and less entertaining account can be found in Verster et al. (Journal of Sleep Research, 2011 20:585-8). The experiment measured how often drivers weaved on a straight road after several hours of driving. It was found that the fatigue caused by 3 hours of driving exceeded the impairment of 0.08% blood alcohol content. 0.08% is the definition of drunk driving in the USA.

Your *circadian rhythms* make you especially sleepy in the afternoon and when it gets dark. So these are the times you need to be especially careful if you're driving.

Napping

Track driving is even more fatiguing than street driving. Make sure you get a lot of rest the night before a track event. In addition, taking a short nap between sessions can be surprisingly effective. In Episode 198, "Crab Napping", the MythBusters measured various motor skills and intellectual challenges while fully rested, after 30 hours awake, and taking 20 minute naps every 6 hours. After 30 hours, a few naps doesn't restore you completely, but it's far superior to not sleeping at all. Similarly, NASA researchers found that pilots benefit from a 40 minute nap (Rosekind et al., Journal of Sleep Research 1995 S2:62-66). Also, napping is more effective than caffeine for restoring motor skills (Mednick et al., Behavioural Brain Research 193:79-86).

How long should your nap be? A very short nap, even less than 10 minutes is beneficial. Longer naps appear to keep you refreshed longer, but they also take longer to recover from. *Sleep inertia* is the prolonged groggy feeling you experience after a deep sleep. If you need to be active immediately after your nap, make it short (10-20 minutes). If you can get some post-nap recovery time, take a longer nap.

36792035R00066